The Perennial Philosophy
Series

World Wisdom
The Library of Perennial Philosophy

The Library of Perennial Philosophy is dedicated to the exposition of the timeless Truth underlying the diverse religions. This Truth, often referred to as the Sophia Perennis—or Perennial Wisdom—finds its expression in the revealed Scriptures as well as the writings of the great sages and the artistic creations of the traditional worlds.

Men of a Single Book: Fundamentalism in Islam, Christianity, and Modern Thought appears as one of our selections in the Perennial Philosophy series.

The Perennial Philosophy Series

In the beginning of the twentieth century, a school of thought arose which has focused on the enunciation and explanation of the Perennial Philosophy. Deeply rooted in the sense of the sacred, the writings of its leading exponents establish an indispensable foundation for understanding the timeless Truth and spiritual practices which live in the heart of all religions. Some of these titles are companion volumes to the Treasures of the World's Religions series, which allows a comparison of the writings of the great sages of the past with the perennialist authors of our time.

Cover:
Miniature from an Ethiopian Evangeliary, c. 1700

Men of a Single Book

Fundamentalism in Islam, Christianity, and Modern Thought

by

MATEUS SOARES DE AZEVEDO

Foreword by

ALBERTO VASCONCELLOS QUEIROZ

Introduction by

WILLIAM STODDART

World Wisdom

Men of a Single Book:
Fundamentalism in Islam, Christianity, and Modern Thought
© 2010 World Wisdom, Inc.

Originally published in Portuguese as
Homens de um Livro só,
Editora Best Seller, 2008.
Revised and enlarged for this World Wisdom edition.

Library of Congress Cataloging-in-Publication Data

Azevedo, Mateus Soares de, 1959-
  Men of a single book : fundamentalism in Islam, Christianity, and
modern thought / by Mateus Soares de Azevedo ; foreword by
Alberto Vasconcellos Queiroz ; introduction by William Stoddart.
      p. cm. -- (The perennial philosophy series)
  Includes bibliographical references (p.   ) and index.
  ISBN 978-1-935493-18-1 (pbk. : alk. paper) 1. Religious funda-
mentalism. 2. Ideology--Religious aspects. 3. Religion--Philosophy.
4. Tradition (Philosophy) I. Title.
  BL238.A997 2010
  200.9'04--dc22
                                                        2010029201

Printed on acid-free paper in the United States of America

For information address World Wisdom, Inc.
P.O. Box 2682, Bloomington, Indiana 47402-2682
www.worldwisdom.com

CONTENTS

FOREWORD

According to an ancient tradition, Saint Thomas Aquinas once said: "I fear the man of a single book" (*timeo hominem unius libri*). Over the centuries, this saying has been interpreted in two ways. On the one hand, it has been understood to mean that, for the man who applies himself to the thorough study of a (good) book, the knowledge that he thus acquires will serve as a basis and a key for the effective understanding of other ideas—contrarily to what happens when a man studies many books, but superficially, and is left with an unorganized and poor comprehension of the diverse concepts and ideas which they present.

On the other hand, the same saying has been envisaged as meaning that the man of a single book is one who encloses himself emotionally in a single point of view, refusing to cultivate objectivity, to give priority to intelligence, or to put himself in the place of another.

In *Men of a Single Book: Fundamentalism in Islam, Christianity, and Modern Thought*, Mateus Soares de Azevedo uses the expression "men of a single book" in this second sense to depict, in a direct and concrete manner, what the main characteristic of militant fundamentalism is. Of course, the term "book" is not taken here in its literal sense, but as an equivalent of "point of view". Fundamentalism is then the emotional enslavement of men to a particular point of view, coupled with a violent affirmation of it and an equally violent rejection of any contrary ideas.

Building on a comprehensive knowledge of the Islamic universe and a solid acquaintance with the best traditional and academic sources, the author does not hesitate to say that Islamic fundamentalism is diametrically opposed to the true spirit of Muhammad's religion. This will obviously come as a surprise to many readers, but Soares de Azevedo explains to us that fundamentalists are really guided by modernistic and nationalistic ideas and influences, religion being in all this only a superficial veneer. Authentic Islam, in fact, is a tradition of tolerance, which is historically proved by centuries of peaceful relations between Muslims, Christians, and Jews in medieval Spain or, in a later period, under the Ottoman Empire.

In order to offer the reader a necessary minimum understanding of the true nature of Islam, the author makes a series of enlightened comparisons between this religion and Christianity, between the Koran and the Bible, between Jesus and Muhammad. (An important specific: following a lesson drawn from the books of Frithjof Schuon, Azevedo explains to us that the Islamic counterpart of Jesus Christ—the "Word made Man"—is not the Prophet Muhammad, but the Holy Koran—the "Word made Book".)

Besides Islamic fundamentalism, the author uses the term fundamentalism to define other conflicts in which the fundamental error is always the emotional and violent attachment to a biased, superficial, and non-traditional idea of religion, an idea which, in fact, serves an extremist political ideology.

Last but not least, Soares de Azevedo discusses what he calls "anti-religious fundamentalism". Marxism, Psychoanalysis, and Darwinian transformist evolution, for example, fall into this category, for they too are characterized by an emotional and blind attachment to an idea or set of ideas, by the dogmatic refusal to accept that these ideas can be wrong or relative, or that opposite ideas can also be valid. These anti-religious fundamentalisms, the author tells us, are as pernicious and harmful as the religious fundamentalisms, or even more so.

Men of a Single Book is a lucid and independent work which raises important questions about the contemporary world, and provides us with striking answers to these questions.

—Alberto Vasconcellos Queiroz

INTRODUCTION

If one wished to sum up in one word the central evil of the modern age, one could do so with the word "atheism". While this diagnosis might command ready agreement on the part of religiously-minded people, it might still, because it seems too abstract or too general, be regarded as a trifle facile. Nevertheless, I believe that, in one or more of its many guises, it is precisely atheism that is at the root of all modern evils. Atheism may be as ancient as fallen man, but the atheism that is with us today has its direct origin in the ideas of the eighteenth-century "enlightenment"—the ideas espoused by Voltaire, Rousseau, and the *encylopédistes*.

Of course, I use the term "atheism" in an extremely comprehensive way, and I include in it things not usually perceived as being directly atheistic, such as illogic, unimaginativeness, indifference, and complacency—all so many denials of God (and thus so many abdications of humanity) without which such absurd but successful hoaxes as evolutionism, psychologism, and marxism would never have been possible.

In the twentieth century, the most explicit and brutal form of atheism was Soviet communism. In 1991, after more than seventy years of cruel oppression and persecution—during which it enjoyed the enthusiastic approval of "enlightened" academia—it foundered in a really big way. Needless to say, the evil and the ignorance that took concrete form in communism have not simply evaporated. They have, alas, found other forms of expression.

When something is perceived as bad, there are usually reactions to it, and these in turn can be either good or bad. There was the reaction to worldliness of St. Francis of Assisi, a "second Christ" (*alter Christus*) who, through the strength of his faith and his asceticism, reanimated and reinvigorated the Christian tradition for centuries to come. One could perhaps think of other renewals of this kind, but such reactions to the bad are rare indeed. Nowadays, most reactions to what is perceived as evil are themselves evil: they are reactions, not *par en haut* ("by the upward path"), but *par en bas* ("by the downward path"). It is as if the devil took charge of the reactions against his own work—and used them to his further advantage.

Examples of bad reactions to atheism or secularism are not hard to find. In keeping with the age we live in, they are invariably forms of collectivism of one sort or another. Collectivism means the generation of quantitative power from below. Its opposite is spontaneous submission to qualitative power from above. This latter involves individual responsibility and the ability to recognize legitimate authority. In the past, people *submitted* to the self-evident truths of religion; today (apart from the widespread atheism just referred to) there are a variety of mass movements which espouse the *outward trappings* of religion. Khomeiniism (Iran) and Qadhafiism (Libya) are cases in point. So are the aggressive nationalisms of otherwise spiritually-minded communities such as Hindu India, Serbia, and a number of others. This form of collectivism, since it is "religious", may be called "denominationalism".

Like other collectivisms, denominationalism is anything but eirenic; it is the direct source of a viciously aggressive competitiveness between religious and cultural communities, which is properly known as "communalism"—a term that was first used in this sense in India. Communalism, in the form of inter-religious conflict, has today become a worldwide epidemic. But do we know its exact nature? It is the rivalry, to the death, of two neighboring *religious* nationalisms. We have been witnesses to the war between Azerbaijanis and Armenians, and to the war between Roman Catholic Croats and Eastern Orthodox Serbs. (Each of the two last-mentioned rival ethnicities has contributed cruelly to the tragic destruction of largely Muslim Bosnia, and particularly the historic cities of Sarajevo and Mostar.) In Sri Lanka the communal rivalry is between Buddhists and Hindus, in the Panjab between Hindus and Sikhs, in Ayodhya and elsewhere in India it is between Hindus and Muslims, in Cyprus between Greeks and Turks, and in Northern Ireland between Catholics and Protestants. Each grouping adheres to its denomination and its culture in a passionate but nevertheless superficial and formalistic way, and in a manner which lethally challenges a neighboring and equally superficial and formalistic cultural loyalty. These groupings are often called fundamentalist, but in their ideology they are invariably modern, progressivist, and collectivist. Communalism has been well described as "collective egoism". The last thing that one expects to find in these fanatical groupings is spirituality or piety. Not the Inward, but the outward in its most brutal and superficial mode, is their concern. They defend the form while killing the essence; they will kill for the husk, while trampling on the life-giving kernel. They kill not only their putative religious rival: they have already killed themselves. Communalism, like all shallow—but consuming—passion, is suicidal.

In recent years, the most notorious form of this evil has been what is daubed "Islamic" terrorism. This has given rise to the widespread espousal of the misleading "clash of civilizations" theory. There is no denying that the terrorists come from Islamic countries, but they have broken injunction after injunction of the Koran and of Muhammad. Their main achievement has been to create the "Islamophobia" which today is prevalent everywhere in the West. It is therefore inaccurate to think in terms of a "clash of civilizations"; it is rather a clash between modern urban terrorism (wrongly called "Islamic") and modern western humanism (wrongly called "Christian"). It is important to understand that there is today no necessary clash between traditional Islam and traditional Christianity. Indeed, in a world that is increasingly unprincipled[1] and forgetful of

---

[1] Or, more precisely, a world that slavishly follows the pseudo-principles

God, the two ancient religions are actually on the same side.

It might be said that one can find a prefiguration of communalism in the "holy wars" of ages past—the Crusades, for example—in which two traditional systems were pitted against one another, each one viewing the other as the representative of evil. It is a far cry, however, from the holy wars, chivalric or otherwise, of the Middle Ages and the mindless hatreds and mechanized exterminations of modern times.

There is no doubt, however, that the seismic "crack" or "fault" which runs through former Yugoslavia, Ukraine, and elsewhere in Eastern Europe does have its origin in an ancient division, namely, the "Great Schism" of A.D. 1054. It is the dividing line between Eastern and Western Christendom. I doubt if there is any more bitterly-manned frontier in the whole world. This is a chilling reminder in the contemporary Western climate of facile and superficial ecumenism.

In view of the ancient origin of most of the present-day communal divisions, it could perhaps be objected that communalism is no more than the instinct of self-preservation, and that, as such, it is as old as mankind. However, this is far from being the case. For very many centuries, the world was divided into great empires, each comprising a variety of peoples and often a variety of religions. The Anglo-Greek traveler and author Marco Pallis once made mention of an 18th century Tibetan book which (from the standpoint of Tibet) referred to the four great empires, which to them seemed to encompass the world: the Chinese, the Mughal, the Russian, and the Roman. By this last term they meant Christendom or Europe.

It was at the end of World War I that several empires that had encompassed many different peoples and religions crumbled: the Prussian, the Austro-Hungarian, the Ottoman. Many new countries appeared: Poland, Czechoslovakia, Yugoslavia, amongst others. Also some independent Arab coun-

of "political correctness".

tries emerged from the Ottoman Turkish empire. All this required an "ideological" basis, and this was found in 1918 in the "Fourteen Points" of President Woodrow Wilson, one of which was "self-determination", the first time these fateful words achieved prominence. The idea may have been well-intentioned—a safeguard against putative imperial oppression—but it has since become a dogma of the modern world and of the United Nations, and is the "philosophical" justification of almost all current communalism and ethnic conflict. To paraphrase the words of the late Professor John Lodge, often quoted by Ananda Coomaraswamy: from the four great empires known to the Tibetans to the present-day "United Nations", *quelle dégringolade!*

*　*　*

Let us leave communalism for a moment, and turn to a very different phenomenon of our times. This is what the American Academy of Religion has called "the perennialist or esoterist school", also known as "the traditionalist school", of which the founders were the French philosopher and orientalist René Guénon (1886-1951) and the German philosopher and poet Frithjof Schuon (1907-1998), and which was further expounded by Ananda Coomaraswamy (1877-1947) and Titus Burckhardt (1908-1984).[2] Its principal characteristics include the fundamental and essential principles of metaphysics (with its cosmological and anthropological ramifications), intellectual intuition, orthodoxy, tradition, universality, the science of symbolism; spirituality in the broadest sense; intrinsic morals and esthetics; and the meaning and importance of sacred art. A very important characteristic is a deep-reaching critique of the modern world, on the basis of strictly traditional principles. Above all, like Pythagoras and Plato, Guénon

---

[2] See the chapter "Frithjof Schuon and the Perennialist School" in *Remembering in a World of Forgetting.*

and Schuon derive their doctrinal expositions directly from *intellectus purus*—a process which lends to these expositions an unsurpassable lucidity, not to say infallibility.

This supra-formal truth constitutes the *religio perennis*. This term, which does not imply a rejection of the similar terms *philosophia perennis* and *sophia perennis*, nevertheless contains a hint of an additional dimension which is unfailingly present in Schuon's writings. This is that intellectual understanding entails a spiritual responsibility, that intelligence requires to be complemented by sincerity and faith, and that "seeing" (in height) implies "believing" (in depth). In other words, the greater our perception of essential and saving truth, the greater our obligation towards an effort of inward or spiritual "realization".

I have called this perennialist current of intellectuality and spirituality "a phenomenon of our times"—but unlike other phenomena of today, it is a secret one, a "still small voice", a hidden presence, sought out and found only by those with a hunger and thirst for it, and known only to those with eyes to see and ears to hear.

* * *

Returning to communalism: at the outward level, this is sometimes addressed in a desultory and piecemeal way by what is called "the international community". And of course, the United States has become embroiled in a war that is linked with this question. Inevitably, the response to such efforts is highly uneven—experience has shown that there is no one who can effectively "police" the entire world. Such sympathy as is extended to victims is on a humanitarian basis towards individuals. It does not comprehend or consider the value of communities, collectivities, or what we might call "traditional civilizations", be these ethnic or religious, and it is precisely they which are at risk. It is precisely such religious communities—be they Tibetan Buddhists or Bosnian Muslims—that are in danger of being destroyed by a powerful (and sinisterly "idealistic") neighbor—something much less likely to happen when they were part of a large, but tolerant (because "realistic") empire. Bosnia, for example, was part of the Austro-Hungarian empire. This empire encompassed, ethnically speaking, Germans, Magyars, and Slavs and, religiously speaking, Roman Catholicism, Eastern Orthodoxy, and Islam. I have myself visited many mosques in Bosnia, and in several of them I saw magnificent Persian prayer carpets donated by the Emperor Franz Josef. This is a courtesy unlikely to be extended to the Slavic Muslims by the competing religious nationalism of their Eastern Orthodox neighbors, whose sentiments, on the contrary, have shown themselves to be exterminatory! Both Frithjof Schuon and Titus Burckhardt have mentioned in their writings that kings and nobles often had a wisdom and a tolerance unknown in a denominationally-motivated clergy—today it would be known as an ideologically-motivated political élite—who unfortunately have it in their power to influence the people along denominationalist, or inanely ideological, lines. A similar point was made by Dante, who, for intellectual and spiritual reasons, sided with the Emperor, and not the Pope.

*   *   *

Communalism derives from denominationalism. Communalism is obviously outward; denominationalism, being an attitude of mind, could perhaps be described as "falsely inward". There is virtually nothing that we as individuals can do outwardly about communalism; but we can always keep under review our attitudes towards our own denomination, and be on guard against any slipping into what I have called "denominationalism" (which the French call "confessionalism"). We must not, even within ourselves, give comfort to communalism by consciously or unconsciously participating in the denominationalism that makes it possible.

As I have mentioned, the traditionalist writings are largely an exposition of the *religio perennis*, the "underlying religion" of essential truth and saving grace which is at the heart of each great revelation (and of which each great revelation is the providential "clothing" for a particular sector of humanity). Because of this relationship between the "underlying religion" and its various "providential clothings", it is necessary for any-one wishing access to this "underlying religion" to do so by espousing one particular traditional and orthodox religion, to believe and understand its central theses (its "dogmas"), and to participate in its way of sanctification (its "sacraments"). The universalism of the perennialist does not mean dispensing with sacred forms that were revealed by God for our salvation. There is no other way than through these. The perennialist is simply aware that the Formless must needs be represented on earth by a plurality of forms. The contrary is metaphysically impossible.

To return to the *philosophia perennis* or *religio perennis*: one finds two types of people attracted to it. There are those who are already say, Catholics or Muslims, and who find that the insights of the *religio perennis* produce a deepening and an essentialization of their pre-existing faith; and there are those—possibly products of the post-religious modern world—who have discovered and been conquered by the *religio perennis*, and who as a result embrace, say, Catholicism or Islam in order sincerely to live, actualize, or realize, the truth or the truths that they have discovered. The first group are Catholics or Muslims first and *religio perennis* second; the second group are *religio perennis* first and Catholics or Muslims second. Those in the first category already possessed some-thing of value, something sacred; as a result, they may hesitate to embrace fully all the theses of the *religio perennis*. Those in the second category, on the other hand, owe everything to the *religio perennis*; absolutely nothing else could have awakened them to the sacred and distanced them from the illusions of the modern world; as a result, they may hesitate to embrace fully all the secondary demands of the denomination they have adopted, especially those of a communal or partisan nature.

These two positions are to some extent extremes; there are many positions that lie between them. Also, the two positions are not necessarily unchanging. Sometimes a person, who has come to Christianity through the *religio perennis*, slips into the life of his denomination, and "metaphysics", "universalism", etc., cease to be in the forefront of his spiritual life. Sometimes, on the other hand, a person who has been a "denominationalist", suddenly or gradually sees the full meaning of the *religio perennis*, is overwhelmed by its luminosity, crystallinity, and celestiality, and henceforth his sacramental and prayerful life is governed, so to speak, by it alone. When all is said and done, however, one has to say that the two approaches do remain distinct, and each has its own characteristics and consequences.

Let me say here a word of criticism regarding the Second Vatican Council. It is not necessary to be a perennialist in order to condemn the official Roman Church of today; it is sufficient simply to know the traditional Catholic catechism. The discrepancy between the two is striking. The perennialist sympathizes with the most exoteric of Roman Catholics, provided he be orthodox. But he himself is not a Roman Catholic exoterist. The Catholic exoterist dreams of the "Catholicism of the nineteen-thirties", he gives his allegiance to a denomination, to a form. In so doing, he has much justification, for Catholicism in its historic, outward form endured to beyond the middle of the 20th century. There have been many important and remarkable saints in recent times: in the 19th century, St. Thérese of Lisieux, St. Jean-Baptiste Vianney (the Curé d'Ars), St. Bernadette of Lourdes and, in the 20th century, St. Maria Goretti.

Nevertheless, in spite of this unbroken tradition of dogma, sacrament, and sanctity, it is important to be aware that the Catholic Church of the nineteen-thirties had long since incorporated within itself many fatal flaws, all deriving ultimately from its suicidal espousal of the vainglory of the Renaissance. The irruption of Protestantism is usually seen as a reaction against the sale of indulgences and other abuses, but it could also be said that Luther, who loved St. Paul and St. Augustine, was in his fashion a man of the Middle Ages who rebelled against the illogicality and humanism of the Renaissance. The Reformation did not kill Catholicism; in fact it provoked the Council of Trent at which the Catholic Church went as far as it could towards putting its house in order, thus enabling it to maintain its witness for several more centuries. The death blow to the official Catholic Church was delivered only in the 20th century by Teilhard de Chardin and "Vatican II".

Such strong criticism of the present-day Catholic Church may come as a surprise to readers; but the situation was unquestionably foreseen by the last traditional Pope, Pius XII, when he said that the day was coming soon when the faithful would only be able to celebrate the holy sacrifice of the mass on the secret altar of the heart. Many thought that he was referring to the threat of outward persecution, but it could equally well be maintained that his words applied to the impending arrival of a falsified church and a falsified liturgy. Be that as it may, the true Catholic owes allegiance, not to a form as such, but only to the Holy Spirit, only to the supra-formal Truth. The perennialist or esoterist knows the meaning of forms; he respectfully and humbly participates in sacred forms revealed to vehicle his salvation; but he knows that forms are but messengers of the Formless, and that the Formless or Supra-formal, of necessity, possesses on earth more than one system of forms. The extrinsic reason for this plurality is the great ethnic and psychological divisions of mankind. The intrinsic reason is that the Supra-formal is inexhaustible, and each successive revelation, in its outward form, manifests a fresh aspect thereof. In its outward form, I say, because each revelation, in its inward essence, does give access to, and does confer the grace of, the Formless. That is why each one saves.

This reality is what Schuon has called the supra-formal, or transcendent, unity of the religions.

It has been emphasized that universalism does not imply the rejection of forms. Does it imply syncretism? The answer is "No". The doctrine of the transcendent or esoteric unity of the religions is not a syncretism, but a synthesis. What does this mean? It means that we must *believe* in all orthodox, traditional religions, but we can *practice* only one. Consider the metaphor of climbing a mountain. Climbers can start from different positions at the foot of the mountain. From these positions, they must follow the particular path that will lead them to the top. We can and must believe in the efficacy of all the paths, but our legs are not long enough to enable us to put our feet on two paths at once! Nevertheless, the other paths can be of some help to us. For example, if we notice that someone on a neighboring path has a particularly skillful way of circumventing a boulder, it may be that we can use the same skill to negotiate such boulders as may lie ahead of us on our own path. The paths as such, however, meet only at the summit. The religions are one only in God.

Perhaps I could say in passing that, while it is a grave matter to change one's religion, the mountain-climbing metaphor nevertheless illustrates what takes place when one does. One moves horizontally across the mountain and joins an alternative path, and at that point one starts climbing again. One does not have to go back to the foot of the mountain and start again from there.

*   *   *

In this text, I have moved back and forward between the *religio perennis* and the current world-wide epidemic of ethnic and religious strife known as communalism. I have done so because both are significant phenomena of our time. The one is only too outward; the other is inward and in a sense hidden. As regards the apparently intractable communal rivalries, there is little outwardly that we as individuals can do. Inwardly, however, we can help in two ways, firstly by our prayers, and secondly—and as a function of our prayer—by deepening our understanding of the relationship between forms and the Formless, and of the relationship which, ideally, should exist between the several forms themselves. Each revealed belief system (with its corresponding way of worship) is a particular manifestation of the *religio perennis*. It is therefore no mistake to regard any one revelation as *the* revelation, as long as one is not "nationalistic" or "competitive" about it. In practice, however, it can be a difficult matter. How can one, at one moment, enjoin people to be committed "traditional" Christians, and then, the next moment, speak with equal respect of the religions of Krishna, Buddha, or Muhammad? Difficult indeed. But, in some way, it has to be done.

The basic cultural distinction made by the post-Christian world is still between Christendom and all the rest, but this is simply not a good enough analysis for the present age. The distinction that we have to make today is between believers and non-believers, between the "good" and the "bad"—irrespective of their revealed form. In so doing we need not be afraid of being called "judgemental"! Our daily experience shows us that there is none so judgemental as the secular humanist. He judges everything. The only thing is: he judges wrongly—with devastating effects for the community and the nation.

"Judge not that ye be not judged." This is a text that is too easily misinterpreted. It applies to our egoism, our subjectivism, our self-interest; it does not preclude objectivity, still less does it abolish the truth. There is manifestly plenty for us to "judge", and then oppose: atheism, agnosticism, and everything that flows from the "Enlightenment" and the French Revolution. We passively tolerate so much that comes from satan ("rock" music, fashionable "-isms", sacrilegious entertainments, blasphemous art) and yet we think our culture is threatened if someone wears a form of dress or speaks a language different from ourselves. We must be sufficiently alert to discriminate between what comes from God (no matter how exotic its outward form) and what does not (no matter how familiar).

Our judgments must be totally divorced from denomination. We must be able to oppose the "bad" (even though they be of our own religion), and acclaim the "good" (even though they belong to a strange religion). This injunction may sound platitudinous, but almost no one follows it instinctively. We must be capable of the cardinally important intuition that *every religion*—be it Christianity, Hinduism, Buddhism, or Islam—*comes from God and every religion leads back to God;* in these latter days, we underestimate the "other religions" at our peril. Alas, very few (be they Christians, Muslims, Hindus, Buddhists, or anything else) are able to make this angelic leap of faith—for many bad reasons, as well as for one good reason, namely that each religion has within it a verse corresponding to "No man cometh to the Father but by Me".

It is precisely this "absolute" in each religion that makes it a religion, but it is difficult for most people to realize the *simple* truth that the absolute, being in definition supra-formal, must needs—within the formal world—espouse many forms. It cannot be otherwise, despite the providentially "absolutist" text within each religion. To understand this truth, at least theoretically, is the *first* necessity in the present age. But unfortunately, like so many good things, this area has been partially taken over by the devil, in the shape of the cults, the "New Age" movement, etc. One might say that it is in this area above all that the teachings and elucidations of the perennialists have an indispensable role to play.

—William Stoddart

Part I

Militant Fundamentalism

vs

Traditional Religion

Chapter 1

Beware of the Men of a Single Book

> What all men speak well of, look critically into; what all men condemn, examine first before you decide.
>
> *Confucius*

> The most serious disease that can attack a community is intellectual confusion and loss of overreaching purpose, which can only be provided by philosophy and religion.
>
> *Plato*

The phenomenon of modern religious fundamentalism represents both a "siren's song" and a "swan song" for the world's great religious traditions. As a siren's song, it seduces many and leads astray; as a swan song, it gives the impression that religion as a whole is having its last and dramatic appearance on the stage of history. Traditional religion, with its rich intellectual and spiritual patrimony, is being confronted or threatened by modern fundamentalist movements, with their political activism and ideological radicalism. From the perspective of traditional religion, fundamentalism represents a deviation; it is an impoverishment of the religious message, leveling *par en bas* culture, theology, and mysticism. Modern fundamentalism, in fact, constitutes an amalgam of superficial, exclusivist, and xenophobic religious positions, conjugated with modern political ideologies such as nationalism; it is from this fusion that results its "explosiveness".

One of the most paradoxical aspects of the "militant" phenomenon in religion, whether it be in Islam, Christianity, or Judaism, is the unjustifiable disdain it shows for the rich intellectual, mystical, artistic, and scientific legacy produced

3

by the civilization the fundamentalist activist purports to represent.

Christian "fundamentalism", for instance, shows disdain for the literary and spiritual beauty of Dante Alighieri's *Divine Comedy*, and it has no interest in the sacred architecture of the medieval cathedrals or in the subtleties of Thomistic philosophy; it has eyes only for the moralistic and literalistic sense of the Scriptures.

Mutatis mutandis the same applies to the Muslim "fundamentalist". The irate young man who cries against the West as the "great Satan" in the *campi* of Teheran or Islamabad scorns the artistic originality of fourteen centuries of Islamic art; he has no interest in the profundities of Avicenna's philosophy, while the Sufi art of purifying the heart is not included in his limited purview. The same can be said of the poetry of Rumi, the dance of the dervishes, and the art of Koranic illumination. The Muslim "fundamentalist" is only focused on the political and ideological battle against the so-called Western "Satan", a battle that is understood in the shallowest sense possible.

It is worth noting that the Koran preaches the legitimacy of the religions of the "People of the Book" (Christians, Jews, and later also Hindus), while the militants preach exactly the opposite, exacerbating politico-religious passions that denature their own faith and feed hatred. Militant fundamentalism believes that an unbridgeable abyss separates Islam from Christianity, but the Koran teaches otherwise: "And We [God] also sent Jesus, son of Mary, to whom We conferred the Gospel and infused compassion and mercy in the hearts of those who follow it" (57:27).

Another crucial point, misunderstood by the activists, is the *jihād*. Tradition teaches that there are two *jihāds*: the outward one and, more important, the inward one. This latter implies the "struggle" against the soul's passions: hatred, egoism, pride. This is the "greater holy war" of traditional Islam. As the Prophet says in a *hadīth*: "the most excellent *jihād* is the conquest of the ego." But the contemporary jihadist ignores this.

For traditional Islam, knowledge is sacred; it is a form of identifying the signs of the supra-temporal in time. Because of that, intelligence has always been respected in Islam. In the past, Muslim sages rescued the ancient wisdom; thanks to them, the Western world received the wisdom of Pythagoras, Plato, and Aristotle.

Foretelling, rather prophetically, these sad historical developments, Saint Thomas Aquinas exclaimed seven centuries ago: "I fear the man of a single book". In our own time, this alarm should be raised not only against radical and blind readers of the Holy Book of Islam, but also against the literalist followers of the Torah and the Gospels. Above all, it must be sounded against the fanatics of *Das Kapital* and *The Origin of Species*. After all, one cannot overlook the unfortunate contemporary phenomenon of secular, or anti-religious, fundamentalism, characterized as it is by mental narrowness, exclusivism, sectarianism, and an intolerance of religion—a case of secular fundamentalism itself turning into a "religion" (a pseudo-religion in fact). Proverbial examples of this "poorness of spirit"—not in the Evangelical sense, of course—are the notorious works of polemicists such as Richard Dawkins, Christopher Hitchens, and Samuel Harris.

Consequently, the concept of "fundamentalism" addressed in this book is used more comprehensively and broadly than usual. Marxism, Freudian psychoanalysis, Jungianism, and science fundamentalism are included under the umbrella of "fundamentalism", not, of course, as religious fundamentalisms, but as expressions of this new concept of "secular fundamentalism". Thus, as treated in this book, "fundamentalism" is a rather broad concept, including not only religious fundamentalism, but also certain expressions of non-religious and anti-religious "fundamentalisms", such as those quoted above.

There is also what one could term "old fundamentalism", predominant *grosso modo* until the dawn of the twentieth century, and this modality is rather less aggressive than the current form of modern fundamentalism due to its restriction to the specifically religious field. Examples of this form of "old" fundamentalism are Puritanism and Salafism. Understood in this way, "old" fundamentalism is not something that one should condemn intrinsically, despite its limitations in terms of "stubbornness", formalism, and literalism. The violent and aggressive character of modern fundamentalism, derives, as the philosopher Frithjof Schuon (1907-1998) has pointed out, from the fusion of religious elements with bellicose modern ideologies.[1]

Be that as it may, one has to take into consideration the fact that the challenge of intolerance and extremism is nowadays worldwide, involving diverse civilizations, including, but not limited to, Islam and Christianity. One sees, paradoxically, in the wake of globalization, a sharpening of tensions between different cultures, due to misunderstandings and divisions whose origin is in the emotional and "militant" comprehension of the various religious perspectives.

The prerequisite for beginning to understand religion, tradition, and spirituality, especially in its Islamic form, is to cleanse our minds of all the hasty, superficial, partial, and oftentimes frankly prejudiced views through which the subject is in general expounded. Amidst certain distortions in the media, there exists a need to clearly distinguish between fundamentalist Islam and traditional Islam. After all, a good number of the persons and organizations that have been presented through the years as representatives of the Islamic world are anything but authentic spokesmen of Islam. This is the case for Osama bin Laden and al-Qaeda, Saddam Hussein and the Baath party, Ayatollah Khomeini and the "Islamic Revolution", the Taliban and others.

---

[1] See in this respect his books *Christianity/Islam: Perspectives on Esoteric Ecumenism* and *Understanding Islam.*

Some of these representatives are tyrants or demagogues, or both, who use religion for their own personal or political ends. Others are "reformists" or "revolutionaries", or political extremists and terrorists, who have a limited or distorted idea of traditional and spiritual Islam, against which they usually oppose themselves, while nevertheless taking full advantage of when their interests require it. For example, the Baath party of the Arab "renaissance" has in fact a kind of fascist platform with a pseudo-Arab face; it is very far from representing traditional Islam.

The same applies to Osama bin Laden, symbol *par excellence* of militant and intolerant extremism, who, according to Muslim religious authorities, has for long abandoned the contours of orthodoxy. The concept of *jihād* does not apply to terrorism against civilians and to cowardly attacks against churches or schools—all condemned in unequivocal terms by the Koran. Born in 1957 from a rich Arab family established in Saudi Arabia, Osama bin Laden studied at King Abdullah Aziz University, in Jeddah; there he was strongly influenced by the exclusivist ideology of the "Muslim Brotherhood", a militant organization established in 1928 in Egypt which, in some of its branches, and contrary to Koranic teachings, indiscriminately preaches the *jihād* against Christians and Jews, in a clear demonstration of heterodoxy.[2]

In the view of Frithjof Schuon, movements such as this combine in a monstrous fashion, attachment to the Islamic "form" (not to its spirit) with modern ideologies and tendencies. Karen Armstrong has also understood that militant fundamentalism is a modern phenomenon that must be distinguished from the traditional religion which, on the contrary, emphasizes compassion, wisdom and virtue. "The term [fundamentalism] also gives the impression", Armstrong has written, "that fundamentalists are inherently conservative and

---

[2]   For more information on the "Muslim Brotherhood", see chap. 6.

wedded to the past, whereas their ideas are essentially modern and highly innovative".[3]

Besides the need to differentiate fundamentalism from traditional Islam, it is imperative that the religion and history of Islam be viewed in an objective manner. Islam has been presented in the media and academia as having been spread by force of arms. This opinion overlooks the fact that persuasion played a still more important role. In Africa and in the south of Asia, for instance, the religion established itself through the exchange of argument, through the example of the ordinary faithful, and especially through the Sufi mystics. Muhammad's armies never arrived in Indonesia, the most populated Muslim country of today.

In Spain and Greece, countries that lived under Muslim rule for centuries, the population continued to practice Christianity, and was not forced to convert. This means that Muslims conquered much territory militarily, but did not forcibly convert the "People of the Book" (Christians, Jews, and later also Hindus) who lived there. Moreover, there is no civilization that has totally dispensed with the "sword": the spread or diffusion of its message within a given territory was often contested and had to be enforced and defended. Even in Christendom, the use of the "sword" was not totally despised.

Unfortunately, positive aspects of the Islamic legacy, such as its millennial wisdom, culture, and art are hardly presented. The purpose of Islam as a religion is precisely to engender an *appeasement* in the soul of the faithful; linguistically, the roots of the Arab words *islām* (resignation) and *salām* (peace), are the same. And the Koran says over and over again that the practice of religion produces peace in the hearts of believers—the Peace that is one of the ninety-nine Names of God in the sacred Book. Traditionally, Islam is associated with the mystery of peace, both temporal and spiritual. "And God sum-

---

[3] See her *The Battle for God: Fundamentalism in Judaism, Christianity, and Islam*, xii.

8

mons to the Abode of Peace (*dār as-salām*), and He guides whomsoever He will to a straight path" (Koran 10:25).[4] Militant fundamentalism, then, constitutes a deviation of traditional and integral religion. Although it is difficult to generalize since there are various manifestations of fundamentalism in the world, in our opinion the main tenets of Islamic militant fundamentalism are the following: an extreme politicization of religion, often in the direction of a violent change of the social and political status quo, with religion viewed more as an ideological weapon than as a means for the knowledge of God and of self-perfection; a literalistic and one-sided understanding of the doctrines and practices of Islam; sectarianism; dogmatism; fanaticism; a total ignorance of the meaning of the "greater holy war" (*jihād al-akbar*), the spiritual war against the ego, and of its superiority to the "lesser holy war" (*jihād al-asghar*), the temporal war against the enemy; a misunderstanding and contempt for the profound intellectual legacy of the civilization the "jihadists" claim to uphold; a disdain for the dimensions of compassion and clemency intrinsic to the Islamic message and a complete obliviousness to the meaning of *salām* (peace) which is central to it; an abandonment of the Koranic respect for non-Islamic religions, in particular Christianity; a complex of inferiority towards the scientific and technological achievements of the modern West while at the same time adopting modern technology.

Already in the nineteenth century, the renowned Muslim leader Emir Abd al-Qadir (1807-1883), simultaneously a mystic and the political leader of the North-African resistance against European colonialism, regretted the obfuscation of the true ends of religion among some of its followers. Incarnating both temporal power, as the leader of the Maghreb's Arabs and Berbers, and spiritual authority as a renowned Sufi of the

---

[4]   For the reader particularly interested in this point, see the clarifying book by Frithjof Schuon, *Sufism: Veil and Quintessence*, especially the chapter "Human Premises of a Religious Dilemma".

Ibn Arabi lineage, Abd al-Qadir fought against the Europeans because it was his duty and his obligation to defend his land against foreign invasion. But he never felt hatred against Europe or the Christian tradition. One can say that the Emir's combat was in the spirit of the *Bhagavad Gītā*: the good fight is part of the "nature of things", and it should be fought without revengeful passions or rancor.

In now famous words, Abd al-Qadir affirmed the primacy of the spiritual and foresaw the great challenge that was beginning to appear in *Dār al-Islām*:

> When we think how few men of real religion there are, how small the number of defendants and champions of truth—when one sees ignorant persons imagining that the principle of Islam is hardness, severity, extravagance, and barbarity—it is time to repeat these words: "Patience is beautiful, and God is the source of all succor" (Koran 12:18).

An approach such as this shows that the problem is not a new one and that the authentic spiritual leaders of Islam, such as Abd al-Qadir, have been for a long time hard critics of what we now call militant fundamentalism, and that traditional religion as such cannot be confounded with it. A disciple of Ibn Arabi (1165-1240), one of the greatest metaphysicians of Islam, the Emir fought the French between 1832 and 1847, was arrested in France for five years, was released by Napoleon III, and then moved to Damascus, Syria. There he received the Brazilian emperor Pedro II, who thanked him for his defense of the Christians of Syria in a Druze revolt that put their lives at risk.[5]

Another example of this crucial point: The renowned commander Ahmad Shah Massoud (1953-2001), the "Lion of the North", played an important role in driving the Soviets

---

[5]   See in this respect Reuven Faingold, *Dom Pedro na Terra Santa*.

out of Afghanistan and was the chief of the resistance against the Taliban in Afghanistan. He was affiliated with the Naqsh-bandiyyah Sufi Order, but was killed in a cowardly fashion by al-Qaeda commandos. Massoud's example shows that one of the main pillars of resistance to the excessive politicization in Islam, and to the intolerance of the militant organizations, has come from Sufism, which is in truth the heart of traditional and spiritual Islam.[6]

Many in the mass media speak with full voice against "fundamentalism", but in a certain sense they are also "funda-mentalist" when they present journalistic coverage that is in general ahistorical, superficial, and unilateral. For instance, the main newspapers and television networks seldom take into account other currents—apart from the fundamentalist one—that are presently operating in the Islamic world. Militant fun-damentalism is only one of those currents, and it flourishes in large measure as a reaction to the errors and biases of the West's policies in the Islamic world—for instance, its emo-tional and unrestricted support of Zionism. One proof of this, among many others, is the fairly recent origin of the majority of extremist movements in the Islamic world.[7]

Because of an erroneous interpretation of highly symboli-cal and complex passages from the Bible, some Evangelical Christians believe that support for Zionism must be given at all costs; for, in this bizarre interpretation, the Second Coming of Christ will only occur after the "ingathering" of the Jews in the Holy Land, and the construction of the "third temple" in Jerusalem—even if this means the destruction of two of the most revered mosques of Islam, the Dome of the Rock and al-Aqsa![8] As Jerusalem is the third holiest city for Islam

---

[6] In this respect, see also chap. 6.

[7] Both Hamas, in the Gaza strip, and Hezbollah, in Lebanon, emerged in the 1980s as a reaction to the military occupation in these two areas.

[8] The "first temple" was built by the prophet-king Solomon, around a thousand years before Christ; the "second" was built after its partial destruc-tion by the Babylonians, around five centuries before Christ; and it was this

(after Mecca and Medina), a place where tradition locates the starting point of the "Heavenly Journey" of the Prophet Muhammad, it would not be difficult for the reader to imagine what the Muslim world's reaction to this action would be. Besides, the fundamentalist Christian Zionists seem to forget that it was Jesus himself who predicted the destruction of the Temple of Solomon[9]—whose metaphysical reason is Christ's rejection, as a "false prophet", by the Jewish religious establishment.[10]

These religious-cum-political caprices of the "religious right" in the United States, together with the intellectual and spiritual narrowness of some Evangelicals and their highly polemical views concerning the "final battle" of good against evil (the Bible's Armageddon), have led them towards serious religious deviation and fanaticism; this fanaticism is translated into a hatred for Islam, seen as the principal stumbling block to their apocalyptic notions, and a blind and emotional support for the secular and anti-traditional state created by Zionism—as if this entity were the same as the sacred Israel of David and Solomon.

In our view, the basic characteristics of Christian militant fundamentalism are the following: a literal and superficial interpretation of sacred Scripture and of the principles and practices of Christianity; an incomprehension and disdain for the philosophical, mystical, and artistic patrimony of the tradition they claim to defend and represent most fully; a sectarianism impervious towards other visions of the same religious tradition; a non-acceptance of the other branches of the same religion; a modern politicization of religion; and an unsavory

---

second temple that was destroyed by the Romans in AD 70. The Western Wall in today's old city of Jerusalem is what remains of the second temple.

[9]   John 2:13-22.

[10]   See in this respect Victor Danner's highly informative article, "The Last Days in Judaism, Christianity, and Islam".

amalgamation of religion and vulgar patriotism, often accompanied by narrowness, exclusivism, and fanaticism.

As a matter of fact, the very term "fundamentalism" was first used by North-American Protestantism at the end of the nineteenth century and revolved around disputes concerning the evolutionist hypotheses of Charles Darwin. "Fundamentalists" were those Protestants who supported a return to the "fundamentals", literally understood, of the Bible. But in the general understanding of our day, fundamentalism has become an "omnibus term", encompassing distinct ideas whose frontiers are rather difficult to establish with any precision. In truth, one has to distinguish between fundamentalism, collectivism, communalism, and denominationalism, as William Stoddart has done in his Introduction to the present book.

This same writer has noted in a letter to the author:

> As regards Christians, the epithet fundamentalist is commonly applied to members of what is called "the American religious right". Here too a deeply spiritual appreciation of the fundaments (of Christianity in this case) seems to be lacking. It is often said nowadays that, for the public at large, Christianity has been replaced by humanism. In the case of the religious right (or a large portion thereof), it could be said that Christianity has been replaced by a vulgar and ignorant mass "patriotism". They seem to have completely forgotten that, in the Decalogue, Almighty God says: "Thou shalt have no other gods before Me." This also means: "Thou shalt not create gods who are equal to Me." "For the Lord thy God is a jealous God; Him only shalt thou serve." For many of the religious right, the god "patriotism" has replaced the God of Abraham, Isaac, and Jacob."

The above observations although, I think, true, are nevertheless something of a generalization. I do not seek to forget that some, even many, of the religious right are sincere believers in Christ. Likewise, the same can be said, *mutatis mutandis*, in the case of some Islamists:

13

those who are non-violent and wish to be loyal to the Koran, but are gravely limited in their understanding of it, and are thus capable of being misled by evil men. . . . To return to Christianity: I will not spare the Christian fundamentalists the following comment: these people, who (no doubt understandably) are looking forward to an imminent Second Coming of Christ, are nevertheless strong admirers of progress and modern technology! "Science and technology both arose only in Christendom!" "Progress has only occurred in Christian countries!" The fundamentalists do not fail in expressing their fidelity to Christ by attributing to Christianity the glories of science, technology, and progress. All this is quite grotesque.

Stoddart moreover alerts us regarding the important features which the two fundamentalist groups, the Christian and the Islamic, have in common, namely, intransigence, narrowness, and extreme superficiality in their interpretations of their respective Scriptures.

Islamic scripture, the Koran, for its part, inasmuch as it is a centuries-old tradition, has emphatically condemned all fanaticism and gratuitous aggression. For traditional Islam, religious intolerance is an aberration; chapter 2, verse 256 of the Koran unequivocally states: "There is no compulsion in religion." In fact, throughout Islamic history, the "People of the Book" have had their rights respected and their founders, especially Jesus Christ and Moses, venerated. The quarrels between Arabs and Jews in effect started only with the advance of Zionism in the first decades of the twentieth century. Before that, the two peoples had in general an amicable relationship and the seven hundred years of Muslim rule in Spain is a testimony to this.

It is necessary, therefore, to correct the confusion that the so-called "militant fundamentalists"—whether they are political extremists of diverse shades or puritanical zealots—represent the totality of Islam. It is also necessary to recall that one of the most salient characteristics of militant fundamentalism is its disdain for the rich intellectual, spiritual, and artistic legacy of centuries of Islamic civilization.

To confound the traditional religion of Islam with militant fundamentalism would be the same as confusing the high spirituality of a St. Francis or a Meister Eckhart with a simplistic Evangelical fundamentalism. To accuse Islam for the errors and aggressions of the fanatics would be similar to accusing Russian Orthodoxy for the crimes of communism; or Taoism for the abuses of the Maoist "cultural revolution"; or Catholicism for the crimes of National Socialism in Germany. Needless to say, all of this is highly absurd.

Islam embraces all aspects of life, and politics is traditionally a domain of great relevance; it comes practically together with religion itself. In a certain sense, politics is "part" of Islam and is included in it. Islam arose in the desert, among nomadic and semi-nomadic tribes, among men whose main activity was commerce and shepherding, and whose lives were not integrally connected to an organized empire, with its laws, hierarchy, and territory. In this way, the first Muslims were simultaneously messengers of a new religion and founders of a new empire. The immediate successors of Muhammad were the *khulafah rashidun* ("rightly-guided caliphs"), Abu Bakr, Umar, Uthman, and Ali. They were the religious and political leaders of the Islamic world for three decades after Muhammad's death (in AD 632), and had of necessity to carry a sword beside the Koran, the new sacred scripture, because they could not count on the protection of a *pax romana*, which was relatively speaking the case of the first disciples of Christ. The *khulafah* had to forge a new and original *pax islamica*.

If the first apostles, Saints Peter and Paul for instance, could in a large measure dispense with preoccupations of a political, social, and economical character in their preaching of the Christian doctrine, for of such "Caesar" took care, the

Prophet's Companions, on the other hand, could not dispense with these temporal concerns.

One sees in this way that religion and politics go together in Islam, rather differently than what occurs in Christianity, where politics is relegated to a secondary, inferior plane, not intrinsically bonded to the spiritual plane. "My kingdom is not of this world" (John 18:36), said Christ. And also: "Render unto Caesar the things which are Caesar's; and unto God the things that are God's" (Matt. 22:21). In Islam, politics is a "servant" or "helper" of religion, this latter providing it with principles for action, a "frame" within which political action as the art and science of serving the community is exercised. In traditional and normative Islam, politics serves religion; it is its collaborator. The challenge in today's world is that politics now wants to superimpose itself on religion; it wants to oblige religion to follow her own ways, wants to place itself in the place of its "master". It is this that one sees in the itinerary of merely political Islam: religion in the service of politics and ideology; politics as a "religion"—a pseudo-religion of course. This is contrary to what occurred traditionally.

Schematically, then, one can say that militant fundamentalism inverts the normal bond that exists between these two spheres; the immediate political interest finishes by monopolizing in some circles and milieux, religion as the practice of wisdom, mercy, and virtue. In short, traditional and spiritual Islam is synonymous with politics (necessarily "horizontal" and merely human) placed in the service of the "verticality" and transcendence of religion. In militant fundamentalism, on the contrary, the spiritual legacy of religion is forced to prostrate to "horizontal", superficial, and immediate interests.[11]

[11] For a profound and comprehensive discussion of this point, see Frithjof Schuon, *Christianity/Islam: Perspectives on Esoteric Ecumenism*, especially the chapter "Images of Islam".

Chapter 2

Militant Islam, the Muslim World, and the Holy War

The time is near in which nothing will remain of Islam but its name, and of the Koran but its mere appearance, and the mosques of Muslims will be destitute of knowledge and worship, and the learned will be the worst people under the heavens, and contention and strife will issue from them, and it will return upon themselves.

Muhammad

Formerly, the prince of darkness fought against religions above all from without.... In our age he adds a new stratagem to this struggle ... which consists in seizing religions from within, and he has largely succeeded, in the world of Islam as well as in the worlds of Judaism and Christianity. This is not even very difficult for him—ruse would be almost a needless luxury—given the prodigious lack of discernment that characterizes the humanity of our epoch, a humanity that more and more tends to replace intelligence with psychology, the objective with the subjective, even the truth with "our time".

Frithjof Schuon[1]

Islam, established in 622 AD by Muhammad, a shepherd, caravan-guide, and merchant, is now fourteen centuries old and a spiritual way of world scope. The 1.5 billion followers of Muhammad from five continents form an extremely heterogeneous group of diverse ethnic, cultural, and social origins from Arabs and Persians to Turks, Africans , Malays, Europeans, Chinese, and many others. Nowadays, the Arabs, among

---

[1] *Christianity/Islam: Perspectives on Esoteric Ecumenism*, 63.

whom Islam originated, are a minority, making up only 20% of the Muslim population; today, the most populated Muslim country is Indonesia, with around 200 million followers. However, despite comprising 23% of the world's population and having a rich spiritual, intellectual, and artistic history, there is much hostility to Islam, even in Christian religious circles in the West; this is highly unfortunate, especially for Christians and other believers who are natural allies with Muslims against the evils of atheism and secularism and can help defend the onslaught of attacks against religion and faith so prevalent in modern secular society.

Among the currents and tendencies presently operating in the Muslim world, the fundamentalist, the modernist, and the traditional can be considered as the three most important and influential. Despite this, only the first—and, in smaller measure, the second—receive attention from our newspapers and television stations, media that undoubtedly forge the souls of the majority of our contemporaries.

Be that as it may, the modernistic tendency includes both the left, influenced by Marxism, and the right, marked by liberalism. Both are animated by the materialistic and relativistic spirit of the modern world. An example of secularist modernism applied practically in the Muslim world is the Turkey of Ataturk; admired in the West, he was in fact a brutal dictator who prohibited, already in the second decade of the twentieth century, the normal functioning of the Sufi fraternities, which had been operating in Turkey for centuries, and established a forced Westernization and modernization of institutions and dress in his country.

As regards the fundamentalist current, one can also distinguish left- and right-wing faces within it. The puritanical and anti-intellectual Wahhabism of Saudi Arabia is an example of the second, and the "Islamic Revolution" of Ayatollah Khomeini, of the first. Both are, moreover, "exoteric", despising or rejecting Sufism and the contributions of *Falsafah* (traditional Islamic philosophy).

As for the third basic current, traditional or spiritual Islam, it should not be confounded with the militant tendency. This would be analogous to confusing a superficial and limited perspective with the profoundly intellectual and spiritual legacy of the Koran, Rumi, and Ibn Arabi. Here one is referring to integral Islam, including both the *Sharī'ah* (the Islamic religious law) and the *Tarīqah* (the spiritual way); this means both exoterism and esoterism.

The Islamic world is now engaged in vigorous controversies and polemics, the result of the present politicization of religion suffered since the beginning of the twentieth century—with the consequent doses of radicalization this fact engenders. Nevertheless, the religion as such remains above this radicalism, especially in its mystical dimension. In this respect, let us consider the terrorist attacks of September 11, 2001 in the United States: they do not have a direct link with the religion, for Islam only entered in the picture as a kind of veneer, used by militant groups such as al-Qaeda in order to foster their ideological and political agenda. Not surprisingly, many Muslims around the globe condemned the attacks.

In fact, these terrorist aggressions, as well as the ones perpetrated in Madrid in 2004, and in London in 2006, have deep causal relations with the political situation in the Middle East since the fall of the Ottoman Empire, following the First World War (1914-18). And many argue that they are connected, above all, with the Palestinian tragedy following the rise of Zionism in their land, which led ultimately to the creation of the state of Israel and their expulsion—*mano militari* and by foreigners to the land.[2]

Be that as it may, this militant fundamentalism, or political extremism, which is still a minority tendency in the Muslim world, and despite its development as a consequence of the errors and injustices of the Western powers in the Middle

---

[2] See in this regard Ilan Pappe, *The Ethnic Cleansing of Palestine* and Roger Garaudy, *The Founding Myths of Modern Israel.*

19

East, needs to be explained as the mixture of religious positions superficially understood with modern political ideologies. "Old" fundamentalism, which *grosso modo* predominated until the beginning of the twentieth century, was in a certain sense harmless, since restricted to the specifically religious domain and not involving violent political action. But when this literalist view of the Scriptures is associated with modern technological armaments and the "worship" of a single literal truth, of a single book literally interpreted, and the hatred of a single "enemy", the situation can quickly become explosive. In the same epoch as globalization, one is witness, quite paradoxically, to an acceleration of tensions and confrontations between peoples and cultures, the root of which is in a superficial, nationalistic, and "militant" understanding of religion.

Intimately connected to fundamentalism is the concept of *jihād*. Usually translated as "holy war", this Arab word in fact means "effort"; effort exerted in the cause of the faith, but an effort that is as much exterior and social as it is interior and personal. After returning from a military expedition, the prophet Muhammad said to his followers: "We are returning from the lesser holy war (against our outward enemies) to the greater holy war (against ourselves)".

What did the Prophet of Islam mean by this "greater holy effort" or "greater war"? The answer is the fight against pride and egoism which takes place in every human being's heart; it is the war on the ego and its vanity; it is the spiritual warfare. To win this "war" is to practice generosity and humility; it is to concentrate oneself in prayer, without distractions; it is to do one's duty without complaining; it is to perform the fast and to smile; it is to give and to be grateful for being able to give. The "greater *jihād*" is, or should be, the combat *par excellence* of the Muslims, and of the followers of all authentic religion.

Considered by some authors as the "sixth Pillar" of Islam,[3]

---

[3] The "Five Pillars" are: the testimony of faith (*shahādah*) that "There is

the *jihād* is the one most prone to controversy. But as we have just seen, the most important *jihād* is the inward one, against the passions of the soul. The exterior fight is secondary in relation to this one, and, besides, presupposes conditions such as defense of religion and non-aggression against civilians. Terrorism is not *jihād*; nor is it a *jihād* if the battle is for one's personal glory or benefit, or even a combat caused by mere hatred, whether ethnic or ideological. The Koran says: "Fight in the way of God against those who fight against you, but begin not hostilities. Lo! God loves not aggressors" (2:190).

One has also to take into consideration the fact that Islam was born in the desert, among non-sedentary tribes. The Companions of the Prophet (whose role is analogous to the Apostles in Christianity) established and propagated both a religion and an empire. Moreover, they did not act under the auspices of a constituted empire as did the first Christians, who acted within the borders of Roman sovereignty.

In other words, this "military" and political dimension has existed in Islam since its inception, and should not be concealed, as do some authors who want to apply "politically correct" slogans to Islam, and who want to give it a "pacifist" face, superficially understood, which it does not have. But one has to take into consideration that the inward and outward dimensions of the *jihād* are kept in balance by traditional Islam—in fact, the first dimension dictates the rules for the second, and has priority over it.

---

no god but God" and that "Muhammad is the Messenger of God"; the five daily prayers (*salāt*); the fast (*sawm*) of Ramadan; the tithe (*zakāt*) of 2.5 % of one's liquid annual revenue, to be given to the poor; and the pilgrimage (*hajj*) to Mecca.

Chapter 3

Asymmetries between Christianity and Islam

> That which today is called the Christian Religion existed among the Ancients, and has never ceased to exist from the origin of the human race, until the time when Christ Himself came, and men began to call "Christian" the true religion which already existed beforehand.
>
> *Saint Augustine*[1]

Fundamentalist interpretations of religion tend to disproportionately highlight the differences between faiths. However, Christianity and Islam share many things in common, even if fundamentalists are not willing to admit this fact. For instance, Christians and Muslims are both monotheistic, i.e. they believe in one God; both belong to the same Abrahamic category of religions, which also includes Judaism; both believe in the immortality of the soul, in the rewards or punishments in the afterlife, according to the merits or demerits achieved in this life; both believe in the reality of prayer as a method of communicating with God; both believe in moral law; both believe in the importance of the practice of the virtues, especially humility and generosity, and many other common aspects which the fundamentalist approach tends to overlook.

Nonetheless, there are concrete differences which need to be understood in a proper context and without prejudice from a fundamentalist or limited perspective. It is not possible to objectively evaluate a foreign civilization within the stric-

---

[1] *Retractationes* I, 13, 3.

tures and parameters of one's own particular mentality. Nor can one properly evaluate another cultural patrimony without a minimum of sympathy and genuine interest. To consider Islam uniquely from our Western patterns therefore causes an optical error that can only engender grave misunderstandings. In order to escape from these pitfalls, the best approach is to expound and explain some of the main asymmetries that separate Islam from Christianity.

Both traditions belong to the category of the Semitic Monotheisms of Abrahamic origin; they share, therefore, in a series of key-ideas. Among them, the belief in the existence of an essential Truth, perennial and universal, which does not change according to historical and social contingencies; the belief in one single Divinity, creator of the Universe and of everything in it, including men; of the omnipotence and omniscience of this unique God; the idea of the profound purpose of human existence, including the spiritual meaning of suffering; the belief in the necessity of the virtues, above all generosity and humility; among others. Both religions also partake of the conception of the soul's immortality and, therefore, of a "next world" in which man's actions and intentions will be rewarded or punished, and where indifference towards the sacred will also be taken into account.

Notwithstanding all these equivalences in what concerns their intellectual and spiritual foundations, there are asymmetries that one must take into account. One of the most important of these asymmetries refers to their respective internal structurings. While Islam possesses an exoteric dimension (outward, institutional, legal) clearly established since the revelation's origin, namely the *Sharī'ah* or Islamic law, Christianity does not possess such an exoteric "birth mark". This means that Jesus did not bring—as did Muhammad and also Moses—a social law, but spiritual doctrines and precepts. In the Sermon of the Mount, the inspired synthesis of the whole Christian message, Jesus taught: "Think not that I am come to destroy the law, or the prophets: I am not come to destroy, but to fulfill. . . . Ye have heard that it hath been said, An eye for an eye, and a tooth for a tooth: but I say unto you, That ye resist not evil: but whosoever shall smite thee on thy right cheek, turn to him the other also" (Matt. 5:17, 38-39). This means that the Christian tradition does not possesses a revealed Law, as is the case in Islam with the *Sharī'ah*, and in Judaism with the Mosaic law. This exoteric or legal dimension lacking at the origin of the tradition was later replaced by Roman and consuetudinary legislation,[2] which does not have a strict sacred character as does the *Sharī'ah* and Mosaic law.

In Islam, moreover, the esoteric and exoteric dimensions are clearly distinguished and separated; the outward side is obligatory for all the faithful and is the *sine qua non* of salvation. In fact, René Guénon (1886-1951) once defined exoterism as what is obligatory for all without distinction. Islamic law establishes how the faithful should act in the various situations of social, religious, and moral life, while the inward or esoteric aspect is consolidated in Sufism, which is not obligatory for all and is directed only towards those with a contemplative vocation. Thus, the *Sharī'ah* is the law of action, whereas Sufism is the law of contemplation.

In order to have access to the metaphysical doctrines and spiritual practices of Sufism, the aspirant must be apt to demonstrate intellectual and moral qualities that will make him acceptable to a spiritual guide (*shaykh* or *murīd*), who, in turn, proves his authenticity through the *silsilah* ("genealogical tree" of Islamic esoterism, or chain of legitimate masters). Sufism encompasses certain practices that are not demanded of the exoteric faithful. While music and dance, for instance, are viewed with suspicion by exoterism, esoterism uses them as contemplative supports—among others by the whirling

---

[2] Consuetudinary legislation is based on the customs, habits, and practices of a given people, or group of people. In consuetudinary legislation, laws do not need to be codified in written form as they are non-written norms determined by long-time custom.

dervishes of the Mevlevi *tarīqah*, whose origin goes back to Jalal ad-Din Rumi in the thirteenth century.

In the Christian tradition things are otherwise: there is no clearly established separation between the exoteric and esoteric domains, which are as it were "fused" by the religion. In fact, in its origins Christianity did not have an exoteric dimension properly so called for it did not possess a legal religious code, which, in Islam, was born with the religion and constitutes the social, moral, and religious legislation for the faithful.

Another way of explaining this point is to consider Judaism and Christianity as two sides of the same coin, that is of the same religious entity, Judaism representing the exoteric and "active" dimension (due to the centrality of the Mosaic law with its diverse prescriptions), and Christianity representing the esoteric and "contemplative" dimension ("for the letter killeth, but the spirit giveth life" [2 Cor. 3:6]). A sacrament such as Christian communion, for example, clearly derives from the esoteric dimension; to partake of the "Eucharistic banquet", in which one participates in the "body" and "blood" of the Divinity, is to be present at an initiatic sacred act, accessible only to those previously initiated into the mysteries of the religion. But, in a distinctive mark of its originality, every Christian, in principle, has access to this rite, something which is restricted to initiates in other religions. One clearly sees here a variance in the spiritual economy of the two monotheistic traditions.

The term "esoterism" requires a supplementary explanation in order not to be confused with mere occultism. In its original sense, esoterism refers to something inward, profound, and in a certain measure reserved for those with a vocation and interest in it. Its etymological significance comes from the Greek, and was utilized by metaphysicians such as Plato and Aristotle. It deals with the spiritual knowledge of a thing, not a purely bookish understanding of it.

A second important asymmetry between the spiritual economies of Christianity and Islam refers to the specific place the theological, apostolic, and political spheres occupy in each tradition. Christianity only absorbed the political sphere into its religious mold after three centuries of existence with the celebrated Edict of Milan in 313 AD, in which Emperor Constantine placed it in the category of *religio licita,* licit religion. But this annexation was made as a kind of "profane appendage", as Schuon has written,[3] with the political sphere not organically integrated into the religious mold. In Islam, on the contrary, the political sphere appeared concomitantly with the apostolic sphere, and is totally annexed into the religious mold. The Islamic vision of society's organization is part and parcel of the religious perspective; from a certain point of view, the social and the political are an integral part of the religion.

In other words, while Christ teaches that his kingdom "is not of this world" (John 18:36), conveying thereby a vision of the political domain as something foreign to the essence of religion, or of spirituality, Islam sees the social and the political as intrinsic to the religious domain. In Christianity the idea is prevalent that saints, more spiritually inclined persons, and virtuous souls are not necessarily victorious in this lower world, that they should in fact flee from the ordinary world and that their reward is in the next world; sacrifice and suffering are an important aspect of the religion, following the example of Christ himself. Christians in general are unfamiliar with a founder of a religion who was successful in the battles of this world, such as is the case with Muhammad.

Frithjof Schuon has something of great relevance to say on this topic:

> To Europeans, and no doubt to most non-Muslims, Christ and the Buddha represent perfections that are immediately intelligible and convincing. By contrast, the

---

[3] *Christianity/Islam: Perspectives on Esoteric Ecumenism,* 115; see especially the chapter "Images of Islam".

Prophet of Islam seems complex and uneven and hardly compels recognition as a symbol outside his own traditional universe. The reason is that, unlike the Buddha and Christ, his spiritual reality is wrapped in certain human and earthly veils, and this because of his function as a legislator "for this world". He is thus akin to the other great Semitic Revealers, Abraham and Moses, and also to David and Solomon. . . . This allows us to bring out a fundamental distinction: there are not only those Revealers who represent exclusively the other world, there are also those whose attitude is at the same time divinely contemplative and humanly combative and constructive.[4]

Of Islam, then, one can say that it organically integrates the political sphere into the general structure of the religion, presenting in this way a dimension that is properly political since its inception. In Christianity, the political sphere was only annexed at a later date and in circumstantial mode, existing somewhat apart from the religious dimension and as a kind of profane complement.[5]

If in Islam the apostolic and political spheres go together, in Christianity this occurs with the apostolic and the theological spheres. Saint Paul was at one and the same time an extraordinary apostle—in the sense of preaching the new faith—and a notable theologian, being in fact the first great formulator of Christian theology. In Islam, the theological sphere only arose later, after the consolidation of the nascent Muslim civilization.

In Islam, as in the majority of religions, the message is everything; in Christianity, it is the messenger who has priority.[6]

---

[4]   *Understanding Islam*, 103.
[5]   For a comprehensive and original explanation of this point, see the already quoted *Christianity/Islam*, especially the chapter "Images of Islam".
[6]   The following sentences that deal with the differences of perspective between Islam and Christianity were culled from the works of Frithjof Schuon.

The point of departure in Islam is not the love of God, as is the case in Christianity, but obedience to the revealed law (*Sharī'ah*). While the Christian says: love God and, in consequence, obey His commandments, the Muslim will say: obey the law and, God-willing, till the point of loving Him. Islam bases itself on a book, the Koran, taken by theology as simultaneously uncreated and created ("The Word was made book"); Christianity is based on a person, Jesus Christ, simultaneously Divine and human ("The Word was made flesh").

Islam emphasizes the essential nature of God, the saving Truth of the one God, while Christianity emphasizes the divine humanity of Christ, God's saving Presence among men. In Islam, God does not manifest Himself in a human form; He makes known what He is and what He wants.

Christianity presents itself as a new and unprecedented spiritual possibility, while Islam presents itself as a restoration of primordial religion and of primordial monotheism; it excludes *a priori* the cult of novelty. What predominates is the restoration of an old and in fact perennial idea; Islam makes the return to the "primordial pact" of man with God and to the essential truth; its conception is non-historical and cyclical; it does not depend upon a single historical fact, as happens in Christianity. At least this is the predominant vision in ordinary Christian theology—but, as the epigraph to this chapter indicates, there have always been those like Saint Augustine who expounded a different vision. In this respect one can risk saying that the author of the *Confessions* and *The City of God* presented, centuries before Islam, a kind of "Islamic" (or, in this sense, Platonic) vision of Christianity.

As Schuon has written:

> Islam has perpetuated up until our times the Biblical world which Christianity, once it had been Europeanized, could no longer represent; without Islam, Catholicism would have soon invaded all of the Middle East and this

would have involved the destruction of Orthodoxy and other Eastern Churches, and the Romanization—thus the Europeanization—of our world up to the borders of India; the Biblical world would have been dead. One can say that Islam had the providential role of arresting time—thus of excluding Europe—in the Biblical part of the globe and of stabilizing, while universalizing, the world of Abraham, which was also that of Jesus; Judaism having emigrated and been dispersed, and Christianity having been Romanized, Hellenized, and Germanized, God "repented"—to borrow from Genesis—of this unilateral development, and out of the desert, the ambiance or background of original Monotheism, He brought forth Islam.[7]

It is worthwhile remembering that the much of the Islamic world still constitutes in a certain measure a traditional civilization, for which the next world takes precedence over this lower world; this latter derives its value as a "bridge" to the "real world", but has no absolute value in itself. It hardly needs mentioning how much the modern *Weltanschauung* goes against this cosmic vision for the modern mentality, the terrestrial world of time, space, and number constitutes a quasi-absolute; with its focus resolutely on this lower world, the next world is a matter of indifference.

---

[7] *Form and Substance in the Religions*, 86.

Chapter 4

The Koran and the Bible

How consoling it is for me to know that, all over the world,
millions of people, five times a day, bow down before God.

Pope Pius XII

Another almost inexhaustible source of confusion and misunderstanding about Islam is its sacred book, the Koran, whose
meaning has been distorted by militant fundamentalism in order to justify its politically motivated violence. In this sense,
it will be helpful for the Westerner reader to explore here the
similarities and dissonances of the sacred books of both Islam
and Christianity, the Koran and the Bible, to gain a better understanding of how fundamentalists stray from the traditional
perspective.

The Bible forged the Western world religiously and cul-
turally and we Westerners have difficulty understanding the
profound differences of approach between the Bible, including both the New and the Old Testaments, and the Koran. The
fact is that it is not possible to read the Koran while taking as a
starting point the same perspective that one has while reading
the sacred books of Christianity and Judaism.

To start with, it is worth saying right away that the Koran
is the axis around which the whole of Islam turns; it is the
Islamic Revelation itself. If in Christianity the Word was made
flesh, in Islam the Word was made book.[1]

The Koran—the term means "recitation" in Arabic—contains the essential truths and guidance which molds the lives

[1]   See in this respect Frithjof Schuon, *Understanding Islam*, especially the
chapter "The Koran".

31

of Muslims. The revealed book is a source of metaphysical and mystical knowledge; it is also a code of ethical, moral, and social behavior. It deals with the divine realm and its qualities; the life and teachings of the great prophets, starting with Adam and closing with Muhammad, passing through Abraham, Moses, John the Baptist, and Jesus; this means that the pre-Islamic prophets also have a place of honor in the Koran. It even happens that a Muslim mystic may be spiritually connected to one or another of these pre-Islamic prophets. Of the Shaykh Ahmad al-Alawi (1869-1934) it is said that he was an "Isawi Sufi", that is, he was symbolically linked to Sayyidna Isa, the "Lord Jesus" of Islam, who is considered as the "seal of sanctity" by Muhyi ad-Din Ibn Arabi, the greatest medieval metaphysician in Islam. Shaykh al-Alawi was a fascinating figure, one of the last great representatives of Islamic mysticism, and the founder of one of its major spiritual orders. Interestingly enough, he was a critic of both militant fundamentalism and of extremist secularism, as represented in the Islamic world by regimes such as that of Kemal Ataturk (1881-1938) in Turkey. For Shaykh al-Alawi, the best answers to the challenges of the modern world are in the doctrines and practices of traditional and spiritual religion.

The Koran contains the basis of Islamic law, the *Sharī'ah*, which regulates the life of the faithful, stipulating laws from inheritance and divorce to behavior in public and places of worship. Its 114 *sūras*, or chapters, are not arranged by topic or in chronological order, but are somewhat curiously arranged according to length, that is, with the longer ones at the beginning of the book, and the shorter ones at the close. The exception is the *Fātihah*, the opening chapter, which reads:

> In the name of God, the Beneficent, the Merciful. Praise
> be to God, Lord of the worlds, the Beneficent, the Merci-
> ful, owner of the Day of Judgment. Thee alone we wor-
> ship, Thee alone we ask for help. Show us the straight
> path, the path of those whom Thou hast favored; not

the path of those who earn Thine anger, nor of those who go astray.

Among the sacred Scriptures of humanity, the Koran is one of the most universalist: "Say ye (O believers): 'We believe in God, and in the revelation given to us [the Koran] and that which was revealed to Abraham, Ishmael, Isaac, Jacob, and the Tribes, and that (revelation) given to Moses and Jesus and in that (revelation) given to (all) prophets from their Lord. We make no distinction between one and another of them, and unto Him we have surrendered'" (Koran 2:136). In it, Christianity and Judaism are seen as valid religions: "We [God] did reveal the Torah, wherein is guidance and a light, by which the Prophets who surrendered [to God] judged the Jews, and the rabbis and the priests. . . . And We [God] caused Jesus, son of Mary, to follow in their footsteps, confirming that which was revealed before him, and We bestowed on him the Gospel, wherein is guidance and a light, confirming that which was revealed before it in the Torah" (5:44, 46).

In addition to recognizing the legitimacy of both religions, it says of Christians: "You will find that the best friends of the believers are those who say: We are Christians, because amongst them there are priests and monks, and they are not proud" (5:82). The Koran recognizes earlier scriptures and prophets: "O ye who believe! Believe in God and His apostle, and the scripture, He hath sent to those before (him). Any who denieth God, His angels, His books, His apostles, and the Day of Judgment, hath gone far, far astray" (4:136). "Those who believe, those who follow the Jewish scriptures, and the Sabians and the Christians—any who believe in God and the Last Day and work righteousness—on them shall be no fear nor shall they grieve" (2: 62; see also 5:69).

It is worth recalling that for Muslims the merit of the Koran is not only in its content, but in its form and in its sonority. Like the Psalms of David, the Koran is recited aloud by the faithful. The intent here is, as it were, to assimilate the spiritual power (*baraka*) of the Divine Word (*Kalimat Allāh*) echoed in the Book. For the pious Muslim, the mere recitation of the Arabic text can lead to a contemplative state of remembrance of God, and of forgetting of the world and the ego.

DIFFERENCES OF PERSPECTIVE BETWEEN THE SCRIPTURES

The events and teachings of the Bible reach us within a certain linear sequence, conveying a relatively direct and immediate understanding of its contents. As an eminently historical and indirectly doctrinal book, especially in the New Testament and the Pentateuch, one can say, metaphorically, that the contents of the Bible pass by us as a river: it is as if one is seated at the margin of this "river" watching the waters go by.

There is an immediate intelligibility: one clearly perceives a beginning, a middle, and an end in the Biblical text. It starts with Genesis, which is the narrative of the creation of the world, of the diverse plant and animal species and, on the "sixth" day, of man. One has here a sequential story that includes Adam and Eve, the tree of good and evil, the divine prohibition of eating its fruits, human disobedience, the expulsion from Eden. Then the assassination of Abel by Cain, Noah and the deluge, the tower of Babel, Abraham and primordial monotheism.

Then follow the other books of the Pentateuch, including Exodus, Numbers, Leviticus and Deuteronomy, whose authorship is traditionally attributed to Moses. They contain sacred episodes such as the tribulations of the Hebrew people under the Egyptian pharaoh, the appearance of Moses as leader, the flight to the Promised Land, the miraculous crossing of the Red Sea, Moses' ascension of Mt. Sinai in order to receive the Tablets of the Law and the whole Mosaic revelation. There are also the deeds of the prophets Ezekiel, Daniel, Isaiah, Elisha, etc., and the sapiential books of Solomon (such as Proverbs, Ecclesiastes, Wisdom) and the touching psalms of Solomon's father, the prophet-king David.

Then, already in the New Testament, come the miraculous birth of Jesus, the missions of John the Baptist and the Blessed Virgin, the four Gospels, the epistles of Paul and the beginning of the theological formulation of the new religion. Concluding and synthesizing the whole text, we have the book of Revelation, the Second Coming of the Messiah, and the Apocatastasis.

The Bible certainly has its "enigmas": books such as the Song of Songs, Ecclesiastes, or Revelation, to quote three examples, provide varied and at times antagonist interpretations—despite the fact that in general there is a clearly apparent meaning in the book, and a historical context which situates for the reader the action, the sayings, and the teachings.

In the case of the Koran, the symbolic image one can use to describe its reception is that of a person standing beside a mountain during the night. It is as if this individual witnesses, out of the blue, the occurrence of lightning and thunder, sometimes reaching the top of the mountain, sometimes the planes below him. But the relationship between these occurrences is not clear. The book, then, does not have an immediate and clear intelligibility. Moreover, unlike the Bible, the Koran is eminently doctrinal and only indirectly historical. Hence the need for traditional and inspired commentaries and interpretations of the book by orthodox and mystical authorities. The Koran is a "closed book" as the Sufis say, and only the sages have the keys to "open" it.

There is yet more: oftentimes, two verses, one after the other, refer to different contexts, making it necessary to have recourse to a traditional commentary in order to bring the meaning to light. The Koranic style also causes a certain perplexity at first approach; it is discontinuous, unequal, and dry, as if human language was not able to comprehend the transcendent message being conveyed.

The book of the Muslims comprehends all aspects and dimensions of human existence, from pure metaphysics to ejaculatory prayer, from the rules of engaging in business to the art of behavior at a wedding ceremony. It includes the basic legis-lation for eventualities such as divorce, division of inheritance, postures for canonical prayer, hygiene, military combat, share of booty, etc. Contrary to conventional Christian teaching, the Koran leaves little room for "Caesar".[2] All things are subject to the divine order; there is no concept of a dimension of the Real that stands outside the reach of the sacred.

The Koran envelops Muslims from their first cry to their last sigh: following the birth of an infant, the father recites the *Shahādah* in his or her ears. At the deathbed, litanies are sung, seeking to console and give spiritual strength to the soul in its forthcoming journey towards the next world. All through life, the Koran envelops Muslims from all sides; atop the minarets, the muezzin calls the faithful to prayer five times daily to re-member God.

* * *

Mention should also be made of the idea of religious plural-ism in Islam. As already stated, among the sacred scriptures of mankind, the Koran is the most explicitly universalist. The concept of the "People of the Book" is an idea of capital im-portance. It stipulates that Christians and Jews (Hindus were later acknowledged as well), are taken as followers of authentic religions, and should therefore have their beliefs, rituals, and customs respected and protected. Verses 113-115 of chapter 3 give a concrete example of this:

> Of the People of the Book are a portion that stand (for the right). They rehearse the signs of God all night long, and they prostrate themselves in adoration. They believe in God and the Last Day; they enjoin what is right and

---

[2]   This is a reference to Christ's aforementioned saying: "Render unto Cae-sar the things which are Caesar's; and unto God the things that are God's" (Matt. 22:21).

forbid what is wrong; and they hasten (in emulation) in (all) good works. They are in the ranks of the righteous. Of the good that they do, nothing will be rejected of them—for God knoweth well those that do right.

"Do not hate Jews or Christians, but hate your own ego", teaches a Sufi saying. And Ibn Hazm (994-1064), a prolific and leading author of Muslim Spain, where Muslims lived in relative peace side by side with Christians and Jews, writes: "Put your trust in the pious man, even if he does not belong to your religion, and mistrust the unbeliever, even if he be of your own religion."

Ibn Hazm also wrote: "Every man can be saved by his own faith, in which he was born, provided that he keeps it faithfully." And the Sufi master Junayd of Baghdad taught, in the late ninth century, that the different creeds are like different containers with diverse colors, but that the content, water, is the same for all.

Regarding the Muslim sacred Book, let us cite an extract from *Understanding Islam*, by a Western author whom many authorities consider to be the one who best understands the universal and the particular qualities of this spiritual way:

> Like the world, the Koran is at the same time one and multiple. The world is a multiplicity which disperses and divides; the Koran is a multiplicity which draws together and leads to Unity. The multiplicity of the holy Book—the diversity of its words, aphorisms, images, and stories—fills the soul and then absorbs it and imperceptibly transposes it into the climate of serenity and immutability by a sort of "divine ruse". The soul, which is accustomed to the flux of phenomena, yields to this flux without resistance; it lives in phenomena and is by them divided and dispersed. . . . The revealed Discourse has the virtue of accepting this tendency while reversing its movement thanks to the celestial nature of the

content and of the language, so that the fishes of the soul swim without distrust and with their habitual rhythm into the divine net.... The Koran is like an image of everything the human brain can think and feel, and it is by this means that God exhausts human disquiet, infusing into the believer silence, serenity, and peace.[3]

JESUS CHRIST AND THE VIRGIN MARY IN ISLAM

One of the four great prophets in Islam—besides Abraham, Moses, and Muhammad—Jesus Christ is seen in the Koran as the fruit of a miraculous birth, having been born of a virgin. Jesus is referred to as *Kalimat Allāh* (the Word of God) and is engendered by *Rūh Allāh* (the Spirit of God) breathing into the Virgin Mary. He is seen as the Messiah, the "seal of universal sanctity", healer of the sick and afflicted, and one who has resuscitated the dead.

From the transcendentalist and rigorously monotheistic perspective of Islam, there is no place for a "son of God"; the Islamic spiritual economy thus excludes the possibility of an incarnation from a unique, absolute, and transcendent God. Hence the denial of Christ's divinity, despite the veneration that he receives in Islam as envoy of God, prophet, and Messiah.

Muslims also have a profound and intimate relationship with the Blessed Virgin. Hers is the only feminine name mentioned in the whole of the Koran, and the title of a chapter is even named after her—while in the Gospels the Blessed Virgin is seldom mentioned, despite her intrinsic importance and prominence.

Among the Muslims particularly devoted to the Virgin, there are several that make pilgrimages to Marian sanctuaries in Europe and Asia, such as in her house in Ephesus (in Turkey) and in Fátima, Portugal—this latter takes its name from a Moorish princess named after Muhammad's daughter, Fatima,

---

[3] Frithjof Schuon, *Understanding Islam*, 47-48.

and was in the past a place of *Dār al-Islām*. Portugal was under
Moorish dominance from the beginning of the eighth century
until the middle of the thirteenth century, when it was known
as *Al-Garb al-Andalus*, or the Occident of Andalusia, hence
the name "Algarve" for the southern part of the country. Concerning Ephesus in Turkey, tradition says that, after the crucifixion, due to the persecutions at the synagogue, Mary left
Jerusalem and established herself in a mountain overlooking
the then important Roman city of Ephesus, where both Saint
John and Saint Paul lived and preached. There exists in the
house a source of miraculous water used by both Christians
and Muslims. In a certain sense the house of the Blessed Virgin
in Ephesus is a unique place in the world, a place of pilgrimage
for adepts of two world religions.

Mary enjoys an insuperable prestige in Islam; esoterically
some Sufis refer to her as the "mother of all the prophets". She
is the only woman mentioned in the chapter on the prophets
in the Koran, even though she is not the founder of a religion
or bearer of a new sacred legislation.

As the bridge and link between Islam and Christianity,
the Virgin belongs *a priori* to the latter, but nevertheless
has her place in Islam as well. As mother of the founder of
Christianity, she is a model and example for Muslim woman,
while, mystically, she is the "patroness" and protectress of
esoterism.[4]

The Koran says of the Virgin: "God hath chosen thee and
made thee pure, and hath preferred thee above all the women
of creation. O Mary! Be obedient to thy Lord, prostrate thyself
and bow with those who bow in worship" (3:42-43). A *hadīth*
places Mary besides Abraham in Paradise because she has had
the privilege of being the receptacle of the Holy Spirit (*Rūh
Allāh*).

---

[4] See in this respect Frithjof Schuon, *Form and Substance in the Religions*,
especially the chapter "The Virginal Doctrine".

Chapter 5

The Message of Islam

The best friends of Muslims are those who say "We are Christians".

Koran 5:82

Fundamentalist Islam often presents the religion in a distorted manner and gives the false impression that Islam encourages violence. Consequently, it is helpful to present the basic tenets of the Muslim faith and review several overarching themes prevalent in this religion, which is so often misunderstood in the West. Islam, we have seen, is founded on the Koran. If in Christianity the Revelation is the figure at once divine and human of Jesus Christ, in Islam the Koran is the book which is simultaneously uncreated and created. In Christianity, the Word (of God) was made flesh, while in Islam it was made book, as Frithjof Schuon has remarked more than once in his books.

The Koran includes the essential truths that mold the life of more than 1.5 billion Muslims; it is the source of metaphysical and mystical knowledge, and provides the basis for ethical, moral, and social comportment. Its 114 chapters expound the most universalistic doctrine of all the scriptures of the different civilizations.

As far as Muhammad is concerned, his place in Islam is analogous to that of Moses in Judaism; he is the prophet who received the Revelation from God and who transmitted it tomen; he is also the human model that Muslims all over the globe seek to imitate; he incarnates all those virtues the faithful seek to have. He is the supreme leader, the master, the saint, the prophet, the messenger of God, and the founder of Islam.

Muhammad is the model of intelligence, will power, and character for Muslims. If Christ is the Man-God for Christians, Muhammad is the "universal man", or "perfect man" (*al-insān al-kāmil*), and also the "seal of prophecy", for with him the cycle of the great world religions is closed. Islam claims to be the last religion to appear on the stage of history—a claim that has not been contradicted in the last fourteen centuries.

These commentaries might surprise some readers, as it is not rare to find negative views of the role of Muhammad in history. But this is explained in great measure by disinformation for, as the French writer and statesman Alphonse de Lamartine (1790-1869) said:

Never has a man proposed for himself, voluntarily or involuntarily, a goal more sublime, since this goal was beyond measure: undermine the superstitions placed between the creature and the Creator, give back God to man and man to God, reinstate the rational and saintly idea of divinity in the midst of this prevailing chaos of material and disfigured gods of idolatry. Never has a man accomplished in such a short time such an immense and long lasting revolution in the world, since less than two centuries after his predication, Islam, preaching and armed, ruled over three Arabias, and conquered to God's unity Persia, the Khorasan, Transoxania, Western India, Syria, Egypt, Abyssinia, and all the known continent of Northern Africa, many islands of the Mediterranean, Spain and part of Gaul.

If the grandeur of the aim, the smallness of the means, the immensity of the result are the three measures of a man's genius, who would dare humanly compare a great man of modern history with Muhammad?

The most famous have only moved weapons, laws, empires; they founded, when they founded anything, only material powers, often crumbling before them. This one not only moved armies, legislations, empires, peoples, dynasties, millions of men over a third of the inhabited globe; but he also moved ideas, beliefs, souls. He founded upon a book, of which each letter has become a law, a spiritual nationality embracing people of all languages and races; and made an indelible imprint upon this Muslim world, for the hatred of false gods and the passion for the God, One and Immaterial.

Philosopher, orator, apostle, legislator, warrior, conqueror of ideas, restorer of a rational dogma, founder of twenty earthly empires and of a spiritual empire, this is Muhammad. Of all the scales by which one measures human grandeur, which man has been greater?[1]

Besides being a mirror in which the faithful look in search of guidance, Muhammad is also praised for being able to harmonize spiritual qualities with an extraordinary social and political capacity—these terms are used in their highest sense— for he was one of the greatest statesmen history has known, someone whose leadership and far-reaching vision established, literarily from nothing, a worldwide empire—and this in the space of a few decades.

Islam is characterized by the following essential traits: the simplicity and essentiality of its basic doctrines; its accessibility to the average man; the sobriety and austerity of its arts and customs; the vigor of its faith. The religion, in fact, has as its main pillar the concepts of the unity and unicity of God. "God is one, He is unique", Muslims do not tire of saying. The testimony of faith, the *Shahādah*, affirms the absolute and transcendent reality of the Divine: "There is no god save the only God". It is the *Shahādah* that parents whisper into the ear of the newborn infant; it is the *Shahādah* that converts utter in order to mark their entrance into the religion. This testimony echoes throughout all Muslim cities and villages, as it is recited at least five times daily by the muezzins in the minarets, who call the faithful to prayer.

---

[1] *History of Turkey*, vol. II, 276-277.

Analogous to the Kaaba—the cube-shaped building towards which all Muslims around the world turn in their daily prayers—one can say that Islam has one basis and four sides. The foundation, or "doctrinal Kaaba", is the *Shahādah*, and the four sides are the remaining four pillars, which are the five daily canonical prayers; the fast of the sacred month of Ramadan; the legal tithe; and the pilgrimage to Mecca.

The canonical prayers (*salāt*), made in the direction of Mecca and having as preparation an ablution with water for the ritual cleanliness of the body, are interspersed through the day: the first prayer at dawn; then at the middle of the day; at mid-afternoon; at sunset; and finally after twilight. Total time: less than half an hour. The postures are basically four: standing, bowing, prostrating, and sitting. These prayers include the recitation of the opening chapter of the Koran, the *Fātihah*, as well as other parts of the Koran. The glorification of God, *Allāhu akbar*, or "God is the greatest", is a constant exclamation in the canonical prayers.

Apart from the canonical prayers, which are obligatory for all Muslims, Islam also teaches the practice of *dhikr*, or the invocation of the Divine Name. This is in fact a universal spiritual method, as its principles are also found in Hinduism (in the repetition of a sacred formula, or *mantra*), in Buddhism (in the *nembutsu*), and in Christianity (in the "Jesus prayer", which is more common in the Eastern forms of Christianity, but is also known in Roman Catholicism). "Remember Me [God] and I will remember you", says the Koran (2:52).

The fast (*sawm*) during the sacred month of Ramadan is particularly rigorous: from the hour of dawn to sunset it requires total abstention from food and water for the entire lunar month of between 28-30 days.

The tithe (*zakāt*) is obligatorily given to the needy, and represents 2.5% of the liquid annual revenue of the faithful.

As far as the *hajj*, or pilgrimage towards Mecca, is concerned, it must be accomplished at least once during a Muslim's lifetime, if material and physical conditions permit.

According to Frithjof Schuon, the five pillars have the following symbolic explanations: the *Shahādah* affirms the absolute reality of God and the merely relative—or "less real"—character of everything that is not Him. It affirms, therefore, the fundamental discernment between the absolutely Real (God) and the relatively real (the world), this latter being "illusory" from the point of view of the Absolute.

The daily canonical prayers, and also the *dhikr* or invocation, represent a freedom from the mundane preoccupations of everyday life. Five times a day man withdraws from the passing and the evanescent in order to turn himself to the eternal and enduring.

The tithe is a sacrifice for the benefit of the neighbor; it actualizes the combat against egoism and reaffirms social solidarity. Symbolically, it is a "fasting" of the soul.

The fast, in its turn, is an "almsgiving" of the body; it is another form of sacrifice, in which man voluntarily abstains from food and water in order to strengthen himself spiritually. This physical fast serves as preparation for a more important abstention, the "fasting of the soul", that is, the inward fight against pride and egoism. Applying equally to rich and poor, the fast of Ramadan has, therefore, a social reach, stimulating solidarity through all levels of society.

The symbolic meaning of the pilgrimage is the return to the center and origin, both represented, in the case of Islam, by the Kaaba in Mecca.

Concerning *jihād*, it is necessary to stress that the most important combat is the inward one, involving the fight against the passions of the soul. The outward fight is secondary in relation to this and presupposes conditions such as the defense of faith and non-aggression towards civilians. It is not a true *jihād* if one fights for ideological reasons, or because of racial/ethnic hatred, for personal glory, or material gain.

Apart from the five pillars, Islam has certain characteristic practices such as prohibitions concerning the drinking of alcohol, the eating of pork, participation in games of chance, as well as the utilization of human and animal figures in religious art.

The sum of these rules, prescriptions, and practices constitutes the *Sharī'ah*, or Islamic law. Founded upon the Koran and the *Sunnah* (usages and customs of the Prophet, as codified in the *ahādīth*), the *Sharī'ah* encompasses all aspects of life, be they individual, familial, or social.

Etymologically, the word *Sharī'ah* comes from the Arabic "path"; it is the way that leads to happiness, both temporal and spiritual. Curiously, the mystical dimension of Islam presents the same symbolism of the path. In Sufism, the mystical fraternities or spiritual orders date back to the Middle Ages and still today exercise great influence in the life of the peoples of *dar al-Islām* (the world of Islam). Perhaps the most well known *tarīqah* (spiritual order) in the West is the Mevlevi order of whirling dervishes, which originated in Turkey. It was founded by one of the great figures of Islam, Jalal ad-Din Rumi (1207-1273). Another influential order is the Shādhiliyyah, also from the Middle Ages and concentrated in North Africa (the Maghreb). The principal practice of the Sufis is the abovementioned *dhikr*, or ritual invocation of God's Name.

The historical and geographical expansion of Islam was rapid, especially when compared with the slow progression of Christianity. If one takes as point of reference the beginning of the Islamic calendar, marked by the Hegira in 622 AD, or the death of the Prophet in 632 AD, one sees that only fifteen years after the Hegira, or only five after the Prophet's death, the Caliph 'Umar (the second successor to Muhammad) entered triumphantly into Jerusalem in 637 AD and claimed all Palestine for Islam.

Less than a century after this, Islam had already advanced to the frontiers of China. In the opposite direction, towards Europe, Muslim armies crossed the Straits of Gibraltar in 711 AD, occupying almost all of the Iberian peninsula (present-day Spain and Portugal) the following year. By then, all of North Africa, from Egypt to Morocco, was already under the crescent. The advance towards the heart of Europe was interrupted by Charles Martel, in 732 AD, in the famous battle of Poitiers, France. In Spain, Islam remained for eight centuries, until the fall of Granada, in 1492 AD. This means that less than a century after the death of its founder, in the deserts of ancient Arabia, Islam occupied a vast stretch of land, from the Pyrenees, at the borders of Spain and France, to the Himalayas, at the Hindu-Chinese border.

From a geographic point of view, one perceives that Islam is concentrated today in two continents: Asia and Africa. It occupies, *grosso modo*, the central-eastern portion of the globe, from Morocco in the west to Indonesia and Malaysia in the east, passing through the Middle East, the Arabian peninsula, Iran, Afghanistan, India, Bangladesh, and the west of China.

Today, Asia has a Muslim population of some 800 million, while Africa has approximately 300 million. Islam is no more a "religion of the Arabs", who represent in our time a relatively minor portion of the 1.5 billion Muslims throughout the world. Apart from North Africa, good portions of sub-Saharan Africa, and the south of Asia, Islam has dynamic bastions in the heart of Western Europe, including strong communities in Great Britain, France, Germany, Belgium, the Netherlands, and Spain; not to mention the centuries-long presence in the Balkans, which began at the time of the Ottoman Empire in the fifteenth century. Current estimates point to a total of around 30 million Muslims in the whole of Europe.

In the Americas, the United States apparently has the largest Muslim population, with numbers varying from 2.4 million (Pew Research Center, 2007), to 4.7 million (Encyclopedia Britannica Book of the Year, 2005), to 7 to 8 million (Newsweek, 2008). The estimates for Brazil point to 1.5 million, with Argentina and Venezuela coming next as relevant centers.

Despite this historic patrimony, nowadays it is enough to mention the word "Islam" for a series of polemical images to come to the mind of many of our contemporaries. "Fanaticism", "intolerance", "extremism" are some of them. This negative opinion, as we have seen, can be explained by the anti-Islamic activities of militant extremists, who unashamedly use the religion for their own ends, which frankly are more ideological and political than genuinely spiritual. Contrary to this irrational fanaticism, traditional and integral Islam emphasizes objectivity, discernment, and detachment; it considers the knowledge of the world as so many "signs" or traces that God has left in the universe. Traditional Islam has always nourished a great interest in knowledge; in fact it was thanks to the Muslims of old that the ancient Greek wisdom was rescued during the Middle Ages. It was Muslim sages who were responsible for translating and conveying to the West the wisdom of Pythagoras, Plato, and Aristotle. For Islam, and for all traditional and intrinsically orthodox religions, knowledge is sacred and constitutes the essential element of its universality.

Chapter 6

Sufism in the Face of
Militant Fundamentalism

The saints are like the earth, which does not respond to the
rocks that are thrown at it, but offers instead flowers.

Sufi Proverb

Sufism is the best-equipped adversary of militant fanaticism
in the world of Islam. It is the heart of Islam, at least for
those who are contemplative or mystically inclined. For that
very reason, Sufism is not easily perceptible to the superficial
eye. On the one hand, Sufism avails itself of a deeper, more
universal approach than that of conventional vision; on the
other hand, it can sometimes enter in collision with this latter,
precisely because it identifies more with the spirit rather than
the letter of Islam. It is for this reason too that Sufism has been
the main pillar of resistance against militant extremism in the
Islamic world. This "battle" for the hearts and minds of Islam
can be represented by oppositions such as "profundity versus
superficiality", or "inwardness versus outwardness", with the
first term representing Sufism and the second militant extremism.

Historically, in the Arabian peninsula of the eighteenth
and nineteenth century, the Sufi religious schools and spiritual
centers called *zāwiyas*, the tombs of saints, and the Sufis
themselves were the main targets of the puritan zealots. These
zealots even threatened to pull down the Prophet's sanctuary
in Medina, a place highly venerated by Muslims throughout
world, who visit it in a spirit of pilgrimage. It was with much
difficulty that these zealots were convinced not to commit
this insanity; but they did not spare the tombs of Fatima,

the daughter of Muhammad, and of Hussein, his grandchild, which were razed to the ground.

Sufism has a metaphysical foundation in common with the general religion, but presents, nevertheless, a deeper interpretation of this common heritage; it also has additional spiritual practices. Muhammad is simultaneously the founder of the common religion and of Sufism; he is in fact the initiator of all the *silsilah*s ("genealogical tree") of the mystical fraternities.

The term "sufi" has a somewhat mysterious and controversial etymology, but the predominant opinion says that it is derived from *suf*, which means "wool" in Arabic. This is because the first Sufis used to wear coarse clothing woven from this fabric; in fact, the association of spirituality with wool derives from the Koran, which pictures Moses ascending Mt. Sinai wearing a woolen robe.

Sufism is the best-equipped adversary of militant fanaticism in the world of Islam. Nevertheless it has been confronted by Wahhabi fundamentalism, which has its origins in the Arabian peninsula of the eighteenth century, and which challenges Sufism from within the religion and in the name of the past (though a very specific vision of the past); it is suspicious of mysticism, has a literalist and superficial understanding of Islam, and is properly fundamentalist in the sense of a literal return to the "fundamentals" of Islam, fundamentals which however are viewed in a very narrow way.

Wahhabism has the relevance it has today because of the convergence between a puritanical theological current and a social movement headed by the tribal chief Ibn Saud (hence the adjective "Saudi"). It is therefore a religio-political movement which preaches a strict return to the so-called "primitive purity" of Islam—as if that were possible, for how can a full grown tree with many branches "return" to a previous phase in which it had only roots and a trunk. The founder of the movement, Abd al-Wahhab (d. 1792) proposed a literal and somewhat simplistic return to the "primitive" Islam of the first two or three centuries of the Muslim calendar, and his followers have ever since been refractory to any kind of symbolism. Wahhabism accepts only the Koran and the *Sunna* of the Prophet, interpreted as literally as possible; all the rest is *bida* (innovation, heresy). Wahhabi puritanism has been particularly aggressive towards Sufism, attacking its centers, sanctuaries, places of pilgrimage. It has even prohibited the use of the rosary for prayer, claiming that Muhammad did not use one. On this point, one can respond that although Christ never used a rosary, several Christian saints did, as it helps to fix a rhythm to prayer and is an aid for concentration, especially if one takes into account prolonged periods of meditation.

The puritans justify their point of view against mysticism by saying that in Islam devotion is permitted to God alone; hence they reject any idea of "intercession" accomplished by the saints. For them, a symbolical interpretation of the Koran is "unbelief", and they attach themselves to a strictly literal exegesis. As for the mosques, they must be rather simple and practically without decoration.

This kind of puritanical ideology disdains the legacy of the philosophical, mystical, and artistic achievements of Islamic civilization throughout the centuries.

THE "MUSLIM BROTHERHOOD"

It is important to draw attention, on the one hand, to the relationship between the formation of fundamentalist currents and the development of their influences in the bosom of Muslim societies as a reaction to European colonialism and to modern Western influences in general, and on the other hand, as a reaction to the growing presence of Zionism in the Holy Land since the time of the British mandate in Palestine, beginning in the 1920s.[1]

---

[1]   See in this respect, *The Ethnic Cleansing of Palestine* by Ilan Pappe.

The Muslim Brotherhood, an organization particularly imbued with political radicalism, was established in Egypt in 1928 by Hassan al-Banna (1906-1949), an elementary school teacher. It is one of the main landmarks of militant fundamentalism and to a certain extent corresponds to a voluntaristic reaction to the increasing threat posed by the colonialist Western presence in the Middle East, especially in British-occupied Palestine. It is also an example of the extreme politicization of religion.

In 1949, only one year after the establishment of the "State of Israel", the Muslim Brotherhood already had more than half a million members and around two thousand "cells" scattered throughout *Dar al-Islām*. In January 1949, the organization was blamed for the assassination of the Egyptian prime-minister, Mahmoud an-Nukrashi. The Muslim Brotherhood thereafter served as a model for many militant groups that erupted in the Islamic world. Osama bin Laden, to quote the most famous example of them all, was influenced by their extreme politicization of religion when he was a university student in Saudi Arabia.

From "Fatalist" to "Fanatic"

Now we open a parenthesis in order to comment on a curious aspect of the problem: how to explain the rather abrupt and sudden transformation of the conventional image of Muslims in the West? In Western literature, up until the beginning of the twentieth century, Muslims were viewed as a "passive" and "fatalistic" kind of people, and the terms most used to describe Islam were precisely: "passivity", "sterility", "fatalism". All at once, and without intermediate stages, Muslims have turned from "fatalists" to dangerous "fanatics".

Supposing for a moment that this assessment is correct, we must still seek out the causes for such a radical change. And in our opinion some of the causes must be sought in aspects of Western culture itself, for it was in the West that many young Muslims of the economic and political elite have been educated, both in Europe and the United States. Isn't it plausible, then , to espouse the point of view that, at least in part, "aggressivity" was taught to these young Muslims in the judicious university classes of Oxford, Harvard, Berlin, and the Sorbonne, especially with their emphasis upon "fashionable" modern political ideologies such as nationalism, Marxism, and "third-world" indoctrination? The point to be stressed here is that after being taught about "revolution", "imperialism", "clash of civilizations", "class struggle", "socialism", "political correctness", and much other modern ideological jargon, these young people return to their countries and there decide to put into practice what they have learned. And this does not apply only to Muslims: it is far more comprehensive, as several Third World revolutionary leaders, be they from Africa, Asia, or South America, spent their formative years in the West. It is of course paradoxical, but the conclusion could be that the modern West is in part responsible for the "fanaticism" of the young Muslims, for, as the great Maghrebi philosopher of history Ibn Khaldun (1332-1406) teaches, the vanquished tend to adopt the ideals and habits of the victorious.[2]

THE TALIBAN

In Taliban-dominated Afghanistan it was the Sufi spiritual orders (*turuq*, sing.: *tarīqah*) who provided the main organized resistance to the intransigent regime. The commander Massoud, the "Lion of the North" and leader of this resistance, was affiliated to the *tarīqah* Naqshbandiyyah, one of the most influential of the Islamic world since its establishment in the thirteenth century. Al-Qaeda commandos assassinated him.

---

[2] See especially Ibn Khaldun's main work, *The Muqaddimah: An Introduction to History*.

MODERN SECULARISM

Another adversary of mysticism is modern secularism. The Turkey of Mustafa Kemal, better known as "Ataturk", that is, "father of the Turks", was a prime example of this: in 1925 the *turuq* were officially banned. The criticism Kemalism makes of Sufism is from "the outside" and in the name of the "future", while fundamentalist puritanism criticizes Sufism from the "inside" and in the name of the "past". The first criticism is westernizing, modernist, and anti-traditional.

Another example of incomprehension or opposition to Sufism from modern secularism came from the former Soviet Union—in a certain sense this sentiment still survives in the Russia of today, despite being much less virulent than in Joseph Stalin's time, when the *turuq* were forced underground and its members persecuted as "parasites of society". Resistance to communist brutality came, in the southern portions of the old Soviet Union, from the Sufi fraternities. In the Caucasus, Chechnya, and Central Asia, the Naqshbandiyyah and the Qadiriyyah orders led the resistance. In socialist Yugoslavia, the Sufi *zāwiyas* were suppressed in the same way and the Sufi masters persecuted throughout the 1950s.

THE MAJOR MYSTICAL FRATERNITIES

Established since the twelfth century, the mystical orders offered access to the esoteric legacy of Islam, engendering a certain "popularization" of Sufism. The first of the *turuq*, the Qadiriyyah, was established in Baghdad, then the capital city of the powerful Abbasid caliphate and the main intellectual, spiritual, and political center of the Islamic world. Its founder, Abd al-Qadir Jilani (1077-1166), was one of the "poles" of Sufism. His tomb in Baghdad is still an important point of pilgrimage for the faithful all over the world.

Abd al-Qadir represented two important roles in the Sufi world: director of consciences and teacher; from thence came his tremendous success as a spiritual leader, which started with his sermons in public squares in Baghdad, oftentimes followed by Muslims as well as by Christians and Jews. All were attracted by the radiant *barakah* (spiritual influence) of the *shaykh*. Abd al-Qadir thus started a new phase in Sufism, diffusing its legacy more amply.

He was the one who elaborated a list of "commandments" which is still valid for his disciples in today's world:

1. Do not speak ill of an absent person;
2. Avoid suspicion of any person;
3. Abstain from idle talk and gossip;
4. Abstain from looking at forbidden things;
5. Always speak the truth;
6. Always be grateful to God;
7. Spend money helping people that deserve it;
8. Abstain from searching for mundane status and power;
9. Pray regularly;
10. Follow the tradition and cooperate with the faithful.

In the Maghreb, the northwestern part of Africa, the most ancient Sufi spiritual order *tariqah* is the Shadhiliyyah, founded by Shaykh Abu l-Hassan ash-Shadhili (1196-1258) in the thirteenth century in Morocco. With an extraordinary charisma and vast erudition, the *shaykh* exerted enormous influence in his time, an influence which is still alive thanks to the fraternity he established. The *tariqah* came to life in North Africa in order to lead to spiritual perfection those who live in the world and have professional occupations. Its followers did not wear different clothes from the ones used by their contemporaries—as was the custom then among Sufis—and they were encouraged not to abandon their occupations, as Shaykh Shadhili considered it right to work and support oneself and at the same time to follow a spiritual path. For him, there was no contradiction between action and contemplation, provided that the first was based on the second; moreover, he did not give the initiation unless the person had a job or an occupation. As Victor Danner (1926-1990), a renowned scholar of Islamic mysticism, observed, Shaykh Shadhili taught how to integrate spirituality into daily life, with discernment and concentration.[3]

The Shadhiliyyah *tarīqah* continues to be influential in our day, especially because of two of its later branches, the Shadhiliyyah-Darqawiyyah from the eighteenth century, and the Darqawiyyah-Alawiyyah, established by the renowned master Ahmad al-Alawi in the twentieth century. This latter had a great deal of interest in Christianity, and even had Christian friends in his *zāwiyah* in Mostaganem in the north of Algeria. An orientalist of the caliber of A.J. Arberry (1905-1969) spoke of him as someone "whose sanctity evokes the golden epoch of the Medieval mystics". Shaykh al-Alawi was praised by Frithjof Schuon in the following words:

> The idea which is the secret essence of each religious form, making each what it is by the action of its inward presence, is too subtle and too deep to be personified with equal intensity by all those who breath its atmosphere. So much the greater good fortune is it to come into contact with a true spiritual representative of one of those forms (worlds which the modern West fails to understand), to come into contact with someone who represents in himself, and not merely because he happens to belong to a particular civilization, the idea which for hundreds of years has been the very life-blood of that civilization. To meet such a one is like coming face to face, in mid-twentieth century, with a medieval Saint or a Semitic Patriarch, and this was the impression made on me by the Shaikh Al-Hajj Ahmad Bin-Aliwah, one of

---

[3] See S.H. Nasr (ed.), *Islamic Spirituality: Manifestations*, "The Shadhiliyyah and North African Sufism".

the greatest Masters of Sufism. . . . In his brown *jallabah* and white turban, with his silver-gray beard and his long hands which seemed when he moved them to be weighed down by the flow of his *barakah* (blessing), he exhaled something of the pure archaic ambiance of Sayyidna Ibrahim al-Khalil ("Abraham the Friend (of God)"). . . . His eyes, which were like two sepulchral lamps, seemed to pierce through all objects, seeing in their outer shell merely one and the same nothingness, beyond which they saw always one and the same reality—the Infinite. Their look was very direct, almost hard in its enigmatic unwaveringness, and yet full of charity. . . . The cadence of the singing, the dances and the ritual incantations seemed to go on vibrating in him perpetually; his head would sometimes rock rhythmically to and fro while his soul was plunged in the unfathomable mysteries of the Divine Name, hidden in the *dhikr*, the Remembrance. . . . He gave out an impression of unreality, so remote was he, so inaccessible, so difficult to take in on account of his altogether abstract simplicity. . . . He was surrounded at one and the same time with all the veneration that is due to saints, to leaders, to the old, and to the dying.[4]

An illustrious predecessor of Shaykh al-Alawi was Shaykh Mulay al-Arabi ad-Darqawi (1760-1823), the Moroccan founder of the renowned *tarīqah* Darqawiyyah at the end of the eighteenth century. Shaykh ad-Darqawi was also the *qutb* ("spiritual pole") of his time and a renovator of Islam. He was the leader of a religious renovation in the far west of the Islamic world and his order is still today alive and well, with thousands of disciples from all strata of society, from the shepherds of the Atlas and Rif mountains to sultans, such as Abd al-Rahman (nineteenth century) and Maulay Yussuf (beginning of the twentieth century). Diverse Sufi orders were

---

[4] Quoted in Martin Lings, *A Sufi Saint of the Twentieth Century: Shaikh Ahmad al-Alawi, His Spiritual Heritage and Legacy*, 116-117.

born from the Darqawiyyah and spread out not only through the Maghreb, but also to Turkey, Arabia, and the Middle East. A characteristic aspect of its followers is the one hundred bead wooden rosary, worn around the neck.

One of the most characteristic of all *turuq* is the Mevlevi, better known as the "whirling dervishes". Established in the thirteenth century in present-day Turkey by a giant of Islamic spirituality, Jalal ad-Din Rumi (1207-1273), it still has a strong presence among the faithful. Rumi was a contemporary of Muhyiddin Ibn Arabi (1165-1240), the *shaykh al-akbar*, "the greatest master", and the two allegedly met in Damascus between 1233 and 1237. Mystic, Persian poet, and spiritual master, Rumi was one of the major figures of Sufism—in fact, he was one of the luminaries of mysticism in its more universal sense. He was given the honorific title *Maulana*, which means "my Lord". As far as his poems are concerned, they are widely read to this day, stirring up great interest among Westerners. Today Jalal ad-Din Rumi is the best-selling poet in America. His verses have been used as a means of instruction for generations of Sufis and pious Muslims.

Another important *tarīqah* is the Naqshbandiyyah, established in the fourteenth century. It exerts great influence in Asia and in that area of the globe which was under communist influence in the past. Its founder was Baha ad-Din Muhammad Naqshband (1318-1389), born in Bukhara (in present-day Uzbekistan), from where the order started its impressive expansion, which reached India, Pakistan, Afghanistan, and even China and Africa. It performed a crucial role at the time of the Soviet Union, when it led the religious and cultural resistance to the official atheistic machine. More recently, the Naqshbandiyyah has penetrated in regions of the so-called "yellow Islam", that is, Oriental peoples who embraced Muhammad's religion, such as those from Malaysia, Indonesia, Java, and Sumatra. One of its characteristic traits is the determination to influence the leading classes of society, bringing state and religion into close contact. One of its well known members was the poet Jami (1414-1492).

In the Indian subcontinent, the most widespread order is the Chishtiyyah. Established in the fourteenth century, this *tarīqah* was influenced by mystical doctrines and practices of Hindu sages and ascetics—which shows the flexibility of Islamic esoterism in receiving foreign influences, which is exactly what fundamentalism wishes to deny. Among this *tarīqah*'s spiritual concentration techniques are the emphasis on *dhikr* (invocation) and breath control. Its philosophy received a strong influence from the school of *wahdat al-wujūd*, or the doctrine of the unity of being, developed by Muhyiddin Ibn Arabi. The tomb and sanctuary of the order's founder, Khwajah Muin ad-Din Chishti (1141-1230), in Ajmer, India, attracts hundreds of thousands of pilgrims every year—not only Muslims, but also Hindus and Sikhs.

The Influence of Sufism in the Arts

The importance of art and culture in the spiritual life of Islam is the topic with which this chapter will be concluded. In calligraphy, architecture, dance, music, and poetry, Sufism reveals itself as the vector for the diffusion of the treasures of spiritual wisdom among the people. These treasures can be existentially experienced through the medium of art, despite the fact that the majority cannot verbalize or fully rationalize its impact. In fact, some of the artistic *chef d'oeuvres* constitute a synthetic answer to what Sufism is essentially, as Martin Lings once remarked.[5]

The great mosque of Cordoba, the palace of the Alhambra in Granada, the Qarawiyyin mosque in Fez, the Shah mosque in Isfahan, the great mosque of Damascus, the Blue Mosque in Istanbul, the Taj Mahal in India; and also a poem by Rumi, a Persian miniature such as "the Heavenly Journey", the dance

---

[5] Martin Lings, *What is Sufism?*, 18.

of the dervishes in Konya, and many other manifestations of Islamic art are in a certain way "answers", in artistic mode, to the question of the intellectual and spiritual meaning of Sufism. These manifestations "explain" what Sufism is in a simple, direct, and synthetic way.

Titus Burckhardt provides a precise answer concerning this point:

> Nothing brings us into such immediate contact with another culture as a work of art which, within that culture, represents, as it were a "center". . . . Such works invariably express an essential quality or factor, which neither a historical account, nor an analysis of social and economic conditions, can capture. A work of art . . . can, without any mental effort on our part, convey to us immediately and "existentially", a particular intellectual truth or spiritual attitude, and thereby grant us all manner of insights into the nature of the culture concerned. Thus one can more readily understand the intellectual and ethical forms of a Buddhist culture, if one is familiar with the Buddha-image that is typical of it; and one can much more easily form a picture of the religious and social life of the Middle Ages, if one has first assimilated the architecture of a Romanesque abbey or a Gothic cathedral—always assuming, of course, that one is sufficiently sensitive to the forms of an authentic traditional art.[6]

It is worth noting that Islamic art owes much of its origin and flowering to Sufism. Many of the most renowned artists have been followers of Sufism. The great names of poetry, such as Rumi and Farid ad-Din Attar (1145-1221), author of the classic mystical poem "The Conference of the Birds", as well as in calligraphy, architecture, and music, have belonged

---

6 Titus Burckhardt, *Moorish Culture in Spain*, 9.

to Muslim mysticism. Art, therefore, is intimately related to esoterism, and represents a powerful argument for the richness of the Islamic legacy against those who would view the religion in purely political or militant terms.

PART II

Secular Fundamentalism

Chapter 7

Marxism as Fundamentalism

By their fruits ye shall know them.

Matthew 7:20

There is no doubt that militant fundamentalism, as seen in the previous chapters, is a deviation, limitation, regression, and a reduction to the lowest common denominator of the intellectual and cultural richness of the great world religions. It is a symptom of a profound ignorance, even—or especially—among the faithful, of the impressive achievements of traditional civilizations in all fields of human activity. Moreover, the underlying purpose of this reductionism, by militant movements in the religions, is to serve limited, superficial, and immediate objectives, generally of a politico-ideological character. On the other hand, such an interested approach to religion finds its opposite pole in what may be called anti-religious, secular, or atheistic fundamentalism. The core of this particular brand of militant fundamentalism, which is even more "explosive" than the religious kind, is a "passionate", intolerant, narrow, anti-spiritual *Weltanschauung*.

This secular and militant fundamentalism also has its (pseudo-) "orthodoxy" and its (pseudo-) "dogmas", which aim at being the exact opposite of religious principles. It is anti-religion-become-religion, but a "religion" that totally denies the Absolute—except its own passionately-voiced "absolute" claim that only the relative exists, that only the relative is "absolute". It would be difficult to exaggerate the degree of "fanaticism" with which the followers of these anti-religious fundamentalisms fustigate and persecute their adversaries, real or imaginary, in the name of a supposed secular purity.

65

A historical instance of this fundamentalism is Marxism. At the end of the First World War, when the "dialectical materialism" of Karl Marx (1818-1883) was triumphant in Russia, it quickly took the shape of an extremist and nationalistic form, and even those socialists who dared to criticize such a development were persecuted all over the world, with a zeal that surpassed in kind, number, and degree the most fanatical persecutions of the past. The case of Leon Trotsky (1879-1940) is exemplary in this respect: the Bolshevik revolutionary was assassinated while in exile in Mexico by a Soviet agent under orders from Stalin.

So-called "historical materialism" absorbed the characteristics of the most narrow-minded secular fundamentalism with a dogmatism even more rigid and totalitarian than that of religion. In the view of the perennialist philosopher Ananda Coomaraswamy (1877-1947), Marxism had become a kind of pseudo-mantra repeated *ad nauseam* by its followers. The supposed fixed "economic laws", in relation to which men would not have any freedom, mirror the most fundamentalist doctrines, with its cult of a single book, *Das Kapital* (the single "truth" of Marxist-Leninism) and a single enemy, capitalism. The inexorable character of this "blind faith" regarding the debacle of bourgeois society and the rise of the working class gave a pseudo-religious zeal to the Marxists, with a kind of "predestinationary" doctrine of the proletariat.

Marxism, like its adversaries Liberalism and Fascism, was forced by its own intellectual structure to seek to destroy religious faith and, inevitably, to seek to build a new "faith" based on its own theories. They are typical cases of *non-religions* which have been surreptitiously transformed into (pseudo-) religions. In the case of Marxism, one saw the "divinization" of the working class; in the case of Fascism, the divinization of a state; in Liberalism, the divinization of interest and the "economic man".

Chapter 8

Freudian Psychoanalysis
as Secular Fundamentalism

Flectere si nequeo superos, Acheronta movebo.
("If I cannot prevail upon the powers above, then I shall stir
up all hell.")
Motto on the title page of Freud's Interpretation
of Dreams, *taken from Virgil's* Aeneid

Another example of a "secular fundamentalism", with its
army of "divinities", supposedly scientific—such as materialism, relativism, scientism, and individualism (ideologies which
seek to undermine the foundations of the great religions of the
world)—can be seen in Freudianism, or the "secular religion"
of psychoanalysis.

Much more profound and comprehensive than is usually
believed was the influence of religion, in its various modes
and dimensions, on the life and works of Sigismund Schlo-
mo Freud, who was born into an Ashkenazi family on 6 May
1856, in Freiberg, Austria (now in the Czech Republic), and
died on 23 September 1939, in London.

The idea that the founder of psychoanalysis was a thinker
completely enclosed in the prevailing scientistic and secularized culture does not correspond with the facts. In his autobiography, for example, Freud speaks about how familiar he
was with Biblical stories, even before he had learned to write,
and how much this knowledge had an enduring effect upon
his interests. Even more important, religion was the object of
a great number of his articles, essays, and letters. Among his
books, three deal directly with this subject: *Totem and Taboo*

(1913); *The Future of an Illusion* (1927); and *Moses and Monotheism* (1939).

In *Totem and Taboo*, he sustained the controversial and petulant thesis that religion is no more than a collective form of neurosis—or of guilt for "parricide". In *The Future of an Illusion*, he wrote that religion is derived from human desires and therefore possess no transcendent or revealed elements; God represents only a childish longing for a "father figure". In short, Freud expounded a wholly negative vision of religion's nature and role: it was either an "illusion" or a "collective expression of neurosis".

Finally, in his last book, *Moses and Monotheism*, he reaches a paroxysm in his fixation on the subject of parricide, presenting the prophet of the Jewish religion, Moses, as a *goi* (a non-Jew)! The man who revealed the *Torah* and brought us the tables of the law—a code of conduct later absorbed and universalized by both Christianity and Islam—, the same Moses who liberated his people from Pharaoh, about thirteen centuries before Christ, is said not to have been a Jew by the Vienna psychoanalyst. Furthermore, according to the highly idiosyncratic opinion of Freud, Moses was killed by the Israelites themselves, who supposedly revolted against him because of his imposition of circumcision! It was thanks to the killing of such a "father", and in order to expiate the resulting guilt, that the Jews started to follow the Mosaic religion as a form of reparation. In this iconoclastic "deconstruction" *par excellence* of the "father figure" of Jewish tradition, Freud frustrated, by a mere stroke of a pen, a millennial tradition.

At this juncture, it is important to call attention to the little known link between Freud and heterodox Jewish mysticism, which accounts for the intense exchange of the inventor of psychoanalysis with dissident forms of the Kabbalah—especially with the Sabbataist (seventeenth century) and Frankist (eighteenth century) sects, which, as we shall see, greatly agitated Jewish communities in Europe and the Middle East.

This means that if, on the one hand, Freud had a visceral antipathy towards traditional forms of religion in general, and towards Judaism and Christianity in particular, on the other hand he had a certain knowledge of, and a deep interest in, every form of heterodoxy and every movement of religious rebellion. This is attested by his great regard for Kabbalistic techniques of dream interpretation and his immense collection of idols and statues of diverse divinities that overcrowded his office and his consulting room in Vienna—in opposition, one must say, to the first commandment of Mosaic law: "Ye shall have no other gods before Me; ye shall not make for yourself an idol in the form of anything in heaven above or on the earth beneath, or in the waters below; ye shall not adore such things" (Exodus 20:3-4).

* * *

The long life of Sigmund Freud—83 years—can be divided in two main periods. Information regarding the second period—embracing the twentieth century—is extensive; it is characterized by key-words such as neurology, psychiatry, and science. But, as regards the first period, embracing the nineteenth century, considerably less information is available; it can be symbolized by words such as Diaspora, ghetto, Kabbalah and, inevitably, anti-Semitism. It was in this ambience that Freud was born and raised, and from which he received influences that marked his entire subsequent existential and intellectual trajectory.

An instance of this enduring influence is the foreword he wrote for the Hebrew version of *Totem and Taboo*, published in Jerusalem in 1939 (the year he died in London).

> I find myself as distanced from my parents' religion as from any other, but I never rejected the connection with my people. If someone asked me what is left of Jewishness in me—since I have renounced so many of the com-

mon elements—I would answer: "Many things remain, maybe all the main things".

These words were probably composed in order to prevent possible reactions to the violent criticisms he made of the "renounced . . . common elements"—reference to his abandonment of his parents tradition—but also to indicate that, behind the rejection of Mosaic orthodoxy, there was still a connection with subterranean currents of Jewish mysticism.

Little is known of this initial period in Freud's life, because, among other reasons, he destroyed his personal archives twice: in 1885 and in 1907. What was the reason for these deliberate acts? The most obvious answer is that he sought to withhold personal information and documents that could indicate different attitudes from the "official" and "orthodox" line which he, his aides, and continuators wished to propagate. What is more, the documents and letters after 1907 have been confined rigorously to the Freudian Archives, and are made available only to a restricted circle of "orthodox" psychoanalysts.

Be that as it may, an innovation as revolutionary as psychoanalysis—which influenced a variety of fields in contemporary culture, whose concepts and practices have infiltrated themselves in almost all kinds of activities—could not be the exclusive work of a single mind, as the American author Whitall Perry (1920–2005), has observed in his stimulating *Challenges to a Secular Society*, from which I have taken valuable information for this chapter. And in *Moses and Monotheism*, Freud himself observed that "everything that exists today is derived from some current in the past".

This "current in the past" which underlies the origins of psychoanalysis, is none other than the Jewish tradition itself, above all in its mystical branch, the Kabbalah, and especially the latter's heterodox and anti-traditional currents. Freud's family origins were Hassidic, the mystical school established in Eastern Europe in the eighteenth century. Its greatest figure was the Baal Shem Tov (1700-1760), called "master of the sacred name", a fascinating holy man who renovated Judaism with his mystic fervor and emphasis on prayer, and with music and dance as contemplative supports; but, as Gershom Scholem points out in *The Name of God*, Hassidism was not immune to subversive theses from heterodox schools such as Sabbataism and Frankism.

Sabbatai Zevi (1626-1676), from Smyrna (now Izmir in Turkey), declared himself to be the "Messiah", and caused a torrent of enthusiasm among the Jewish communities in Europe and the Middle East. So imbued was he of his "messianic" role that he used to sign his letters with a "prosaic" *"the Lord, your God, Sabbatai Zevi"*!

Even despite his excommunication as a heretic by the rabbinate of Jerusalem, Zevi met with enthusiastic support from the Jewish masses and decided to enter Istanbul, the then capital of the powerful Ottoman Empire, with the purpose of converting the sultan to his special kind of "Judaism". But he paid a high price for this daring act, and it was he who had to change sides, apostatizing to Islam under the name of "Mehmet Effendi". The frustration produced in the Jewish world by such a fraud was enormous, but the religious anarchism and the rupture with tradition, including the contestation over sexual morality as preached by Sabbatai Zevi, left sequels—Freud being one of them, as we shall see.

In the following century, another religious anarchist and rebel, Yaakov ben Judah Leib Frankovich, better known simply as Jacob Frank (born in 1726 in Podolia, now a region of Ukraine, and died in 1791, in Offenbach, Germany) claimed to be the continuator of Sabbatai Zevi. Needless to say, he too claimed to be the "Messiah", and he too was excommunicated by the religious authorities of Judaism. The Frankist "creed" and "cult" openly challenged the Mosaic law; his "do what you want, everything belongs to the law" was put in practice through "ceremonies" of "the liberation of sexual instincts".

With his theses condemned by Jewish religious authorities, he converted, like Sabbatai Zevi, to another religion, but this time it was to Catholicism; in this way his influence went beyond local Jewish frontiers, and reached Central and Eastern Europe as a whole, where his ideas circulated widely in the nineteenth century, when Freud was born.

"I came into the world", Jacob Frank liked to say, "in order to free it from all the laws and statutes in effect"—a declaration Freud himself could have signed. In the words of Gershom Scholem (1897-1982), widely regarded as the founder of the modern, academic study of the Kabbalah, Frank was one of the most sinister figures of Jewish messianism, a mixture of "despot, popular prophet, and cunning impostor".

Such heterodox currents exercised a latent influence in the Judaic religion, making its adherents accept the illusory belief that they had "gone beyond" the *Torah*. In his informative *Freud and the Jewish Mystical Tradition*, David Bakan says that these currents influenced several Freudian concepts. In his view, Freud operated a secularization of Jewish mysticism, and psychoanalysis can be viewed as this secularization.

But, if this be the case, why can we not find explicit references to this in Freud's work? The answer which both Whitall Perry and David Bakan give is convergent: one of the causes was anti-Semitism; the other was the immense pride and vanity of Freud, it is his "messianic personality", as Bakan noted.

Freud was afraid that, in the context of the racism, latent or explicit, that was in force at that time in Europe (it is enough in this connection to remember the "Dreyfus affair" at the beginning of the twentieth century), if he exposed his Jewish sources, even if non-orthodox, he would unnecessarily expose the new "science" of psychoanalysis to a strong, if not fatal opposition. It is precisely for this reason that he insisted in the anointing of Carl Gustav Jung, the only non-Jew who belonged to the initial circle of psychoanalysis, as his successor and president of the International Psychoanalytic Society. The defection of Jung, in 1913, caused all the more sorrow for Freud because he believed the Swiss would "save psychoanalysis".[1]

Besides, the Kabbalah includes what, for want of a better term, one could call a consecrated vision of sexuality. Among its theses is one that portrays conjugal union as an emanation from union, *in divinis*, between the Divinity and its *Shekhinah*, which is viewed as the eternal prototype of all complementary polarities that manifest themselves in the world of time and space—such as day and night, earth and heaven, effort and rest, masculine and feminine, etc. The opposite, but complementary, pair represented by the masculine and the feminine thus reflects the first polarity that occurs in the Supreme Principle itself, namely, between the Absolute and the Infinite.

It is from this principial duality that derive all the distinct and complementary oppositions that make up the terrestrial world. In this way, human sexuality is viewed as symbolically connected to the eternal "activity" of the Divinity. It is for no other reason than its intrinsic sacrality that sexual activity, in traditional civilizations, is subjected to rigid conditions and sanctions. It is also for this reason that the Mosaic code—towards which Freud as a Jew was originally attached—classifies sexual deviations as being particularly serious. It is not surprising, then, that transgressions of the Mosaic law are at the center of the interests of psychoanalysis.

In this way, though he brought sexuality to the center of the scene, Freud did not innovate. But, in performing this operation, he profanized it, desacralized it, and separated it from the transcendent domain. He thus deprived sexuality of its spiritual aura.

In this secularization, Freud went so far as to "deconstruct" the "father figure" *par excellence* of his parents' tradition, as one can see in the exotic and eccentric work that is

---

[1] Quoted in Fritz Wittels, *Sigmund Freud: His Personality, His Teaching, and His School*, 140.

Men of a Single Book

Moses and Monotheism. In this operation, the anti-traditional ideas of Sabbatai Zevi and Jacob Frank are implied.

Another instance of heterodox influences can be seen in the interest shown by psychoanalysis for the Kabbalistic technique of *gematria*—the study of the occult meaning of numbers and letters (*gematria* was used by Sabbatai Zevi's followers in order to "prove" his messiah-hood). Freud used *gematria* techniques in his interpretation of dreams, in the "free association" method, and in the evaluation of the so-called "Freudian slips".

This reductionist approach to traditional religion—since Freudianism has the pretension of reducing everything to psychological factors and of excluding the intellectual and the spiritual, and considering expressions of spirituality as no more than the outcome of a "repressed sexuality"—has not been restricted to the Jewish camp, as one can find similar operations in relation to Christianity: to begin with, the concept of "apostolic succession".

Christ transferred to his apostles the power to hear confessions and grant absolution—which clearly involves the transmission of spiritual powers. Through a religious initiation, namely, the sacrament of Holy Orders, certain individuals are invested with priesthood and receive such powers. Freud, in a certain way, "adapted", according to his "de-consecrating" methodology, of course, such a conception: a psychoanalyst is only qualified to practice the specific methods of his profession if he himself is first "psychoanalyzed" by an already "initiated" analyst.

Such a principle, that every analyst must beforehand be analyzed by another Freudian follower, brings to light, as René Guénon (1886-1951) observed,[2] the discomfiting question about the source from which the first psychoanalysts obtained the powers they are supposed to convey to others. In other words, who had the first place in the line that passed on the

[2] *The Reign of Quantity and the Signs of the Times,* 233-234.

74

"secrets" to Freud? And so, if Freud considered himself as the first in the line, he appointed himself as the founder of a new para-religious lineage, even if "kabbalistically" dissimulated (dissimulation and secrecy being part and parcel of Kabbalism, whether it be a case of its orthodox or heterodox tendencies).

Apostolic succession in Catholicism goes back, generation after generation, to Christ himself, a religious leader clearly and providentially established; but what can one say of Freud, who appointed himself as a chief of an openly anti-religious perspective—"fundamentalistically" anti-religious one might say—even although he wishes to base his new method on the same principle of "succession" as the one established by Jesus?

The behind-the-curtains meaning of this is that Freud saw himself as a kind of modern "messiah", as the founder of a "religion" without God. In fact, if one closely reads books such as *Moses and Monotheism*, or essays such as "The Moses of Michelangelo", it is evident that he saw himself as a new "Moses", the "prophet" of a God-less civilization.

The techniques of the Catholic confessional were likewise re-elaborated by psychoanalysis, and also in a secularizing mode. The rigorously individual character of the psychoanalytic session, the thesis of "transference"—be it of sins or "complexes"—, the "relief" of guilt, and even the physical positioning of the patient, are examples of parallelisms with the confessional, even if the values and purposes are radically different.

For modern psychology in general, traditional morality is a mere "psychic barrage", something useful on occasion, but more often an obstacle to the personal development of the individual. According to author Titus Burckhardt (1908-1984), this opinion, propagated especially by Freudian psychology, holds that intrinsic morality is the same as purely conventional or bourgeois morality, while the truth of the matter is that the former far transcends the latter. Moreover, in many countries, psychoanalysis usurped the function that belongs to the sacrament of confession.

Burckhardt masterfully explains this point:

> The psychiatrist replaces the priest, and the bursting of complexes that have previously been repressed takes the place of absolution. In ritual confession, the priest is but the impersonal representative—necessarily discrete— of the Truth that judges and pardons; the penitent, by admitting his sins, in a sense "objectifies" the psychic tendencies that these sins manifest. By repenting, he detaches himself from them, and by receiving sacramental absolution, his soul is virtually reintegrated into its primitive equilibrium and centered on its divine essence. In the case of Freudian psychoanalysis, man lays bare his psychic entrails, not before God, but to his fellow. He does not distance himself from the chaotic and obscure depths of his soul, which the analyst unveils or stirs up, but on the contrary, he accepts them as his own, for he must say to himself: "this is what I am like in reality". And if he does not overcome, with the help of some salutary instinct, this kind of disillusionment from below, he will retain from it something like an intimate sullying; in most cases it will be his self-abandonment to collective mediocrity that for him will play the part of absolution, for it is easier to endure one's own degradation when it is shared with others. Whatever may be the occasional or partial usefulness of such an analysis in certain cases, the state described above is its more usual result, its premises being what they are.[3]

This secularizing tendency, of which psychoanalysis is just one instance among many, can be seen, in the modern body of ideas, as the intention to cut off the "metaphysical wings" of man, as Frithjof Schuon rightly observed. Suspended, as it were, between two planes of reality, the physical and the

---

[3] *The Essential Titus Burckhardt*, ed. William Stoddart, 47.

metaphysical, man is in practice reduced to only the first plane by Freudians. This is in fact no surprise, if one takes into account its reductionist anthropology. For Freudianism, the core of man is the id, the animal, irrational, and instinctive part which is hidden behind the "mask" of rationality—the id which is "the core of our being", as Freud wrote for instance in *Outline of Psychoanalysis*.

But the following question is inevitable: if rationality is a mere "façade"—as Freud put it in *The Discomfort in Civilization*—for an animality that is more fundamental than rationality, but which is at pains to maintain itself under check, how can psychoanalysis itself survive, since it is also a doctrine that wants to be rational? Is it condemned by its own verdict, as Schuon sharply pointed out? Or it would be the only one to escape, as if by magic, to this "animality" turned inescapably by psychoanalysis itself?

Besides Schuon, Guénon, and Burckhardt, another important author for whom the contradictions and deficiencies of Freudianism did not pass unnoticed was the historian of religions Mircea Eliade. In his autobiography *No Souvenirs*, the Romanian author writes that "psychoanalysis justifies its own relevance by saying that it forces us to look to reality and to accept it. But what kind of 'reality'? A reality conditioned by the materialistic ideology of psychoanalysis itself."[4]

In *Occultism, Witchcraft, and Cultural Fashions: Essays in Comparative Religion*, Eliade criticizes the "horror stories presented as objective historical fact" in Freud's *Totem and Taboo*—a book which for Eliade is a veritable "frantic thriller".[5]

* * *

---

[4] Journal entry 7 October, 1965.
[5] *Occultism, Witchcraft, and Cultural Fashions: Essays in Comparative Religion*, 5.

The conclusion one reaches after pondering all these facts is that, despite its violent opposition to traditional religion—seen by Freud as a "collective neurosis" and as an "illusion"—he nevertheless shamelessly uses concepts and procedures derived from it.

The principles of the analysis of dreams and of Freudian slips are taken from the Kabbalistic *gematria;* the psychoanalytic session is indebted to confessional techniques; the idea of "analytical transmission" comes from Catholic "Apostolic succession"; the "Oedipus complex" was taken from the ancient Greek religion. The central role attributed to sexuality comes from the Kabbalah. All these influences, or rather "borrowings" were never acknowledged by Freud.

Enveloping or surrounding this entire atmosphere one perceives clearly an antinomic and negationist mental bias inherited—consciously or unconsciously? one might well ask—from heterodox tendencies in Judaism, such as Sabataism and Frankism.

In summary, despite his virulent anti-religious perspective, Freudianism paradoxically attributes to itself roles that in fact are spiritual, such as the relief of guilt and the cure of souls—whereas an authentic physician of souls, in all traditional civilizations, has always been seen as a pontiff or a medicine man, a genuine spiritual guide. These roles oblige psychoanalysis to present itself practically as a substitute for religion, in fact as a counterfeit of spirituality, while at the same time posing as the discoverer of facts that were known long since.

In other words, Freudianism, which, in theory, seeks to put a check on the fundaments of truth and the legitimacy of all religion, has in practice become a kind of new "religion" for the secularized world. It is a typical case of a secular ideology surreptitiously transforming itself into a fundamentalist counterfeit of "religion".

As Frithjof Schuon has written:

Freudian Psychoanalysis as Secular Fundamentalism

The spiritual and social crime of psychoanalysis consists in usurping the place of religion, or of true wisdom, and in eliminating from its procedures any consideration of our last ends. . . . As is the case with every solution which evades the supernatural, psychoanalysis replaces in its own manner that which it abolishes: the void it produces with its voluntary or involuntary destructions dilate it and condemn it to postulate a false infinite or to act as a pseudo-religion.[6]

---

[6]   *Survey of Metaphysics and Esoterism*, 197-198.

Chapter 9

Jung and the Faithful without Religion

> While nineteenth century materialism closed the mind of man
> to what is above him, twentieth century psychology opened it
> to what is below him.
>
> *Ananda Coomaraswamy*

Sigmund Freud was influenced by ideas and practices originating in heterodox circles of Judaism, ideas and practices which he incorporated into the psychoanalytic method, as we have seen in the previous chapter. And if we take seriously Freud's very last book, *Moses and Monotheism*, in which he, as it were, presents himself as a kind of "prophet" who would replace Moses in a godless civilization, his ultimate purpose being to replace traditional religion with psychoanalysis. In a similar way, Carl Gustav Jung (1875-1961) availed himself of spiritualistic doctrines of Gnostic and occultist provenance and even, in a certain measure, of Christian origin—interpreted certainly in his own peculiar way—in order to compose his oeuvre.[1]

In other words, Freud traced back and attributed every human thought and action to an underlying cause, sexual impulses. Karl Marx had already done a similar thing, assigning in his stead the supreme cause of everything to material or economic interests. Freud and Marx were thus the "grave-diggers" of objectivity and virtue, as they sustained that men were not able to think or act in a perfectly disinterested and objective

---

[1] It is worth mentioning that Jung was not affiliated to any particular religion: he did not belong to any of the Christian denominations, despite the fact (or because of it!) that his father and several of his relatives were Protestant pastors; nor was he an adept of any of the other great world religions such as Buddhism or Islam.

way; both were chiefly responsible for the "skepticism of objectivity" which has dominated the Western mentality since the end of the nineteenth century. The point I intend to deal with here is whether Jungianism is a real alternative to this materialistic and relativistic view of things, as is believed in many quarters, especially in modern Western circles.

To begin with, an important statement by Jung from his "Transformation Symbolism in the Mass":[2]

> Psychology is in the unfortunate position where the observer and the observed are ultimately identical. Psychology has no Archimedean point outside, since all perception is of a psychic nature.

This quote exposes the core of Jungianism's contradiction. For what Jung candidly affirms here is that the soul is simultaneously the subject and the object of his psychology. Consequently, all psychological evaluation partakes of the essentially subjective nature of its object. Thus, if the psychic is the realm of the subjective, of the unstable, of the relative, how can it judge with impartiality the plane of the psyche itself?

Jung here denies the human capacity to view reality objectively, in the soul or in the world. What this means in the final analysis is the destruction of intelligence. Moreover, if "all perception is psychic", hence erratic and deceptive, what is the interest of Jung's own considerations? Mere curiosity or pastime?

But, quite to the contrary, it was not in this way that Jung himself saw his judgments; for, quite evidently, he took them very seriously, as if they were the only ones capable of escaping, as in a stroke of magic, from the ruling that "everything is psychic", which he himself had proclaimed. This is the typical contradiction of relativism: "every man is a liar", or "everything is subjective". But if this is so, this verdict

---

[2]   *Psychology and Religion: West and East. Collected Works*, vol. XI, 248.

condemns its own formulator. Put differently: is everything "subjective", save Jungianism? and: are all men liars, except Jung?

THE INTELLECT

"Unfortunately, psychology does not have an external point of reference", wrote Jung; but psychology does have one, for it is from a superior element to the purely psychic that the soul and the world can be understood. This element is the intellect—in the medieval or Eckartian sense of the word—a faculty which is, however, rejected by Jungian psychology.

But what is the intellect? It is not an easy task to define it, especially because in current language it is easily confounded with the mental sphere and individual reasoning. From the point of view of traditional philosophy, which conceives of man as a tripartite being composed of body, soul, and Spirit (or Intellect), it indicates the dimension of objectivity which goes further than the element of purely individual interest. It is the capacity man has of seeing himself with detachment and impartiality, of seeing himself as if outside of himself.

Examples of the intellect in life are our intuition, our innate sense of justice, our capacity for mathematics, our innate sense of right and wrong, as William Stoddart has observed in his recent book, *Remembering in a World of Forgetting: Thoughts on Tradition and Postmodernism.*[3] The presence of the "voice of conscience" is another example of the intellect's action.

The intellect is the faculty that permits us to see things as they really are, setting aside our individual or group interests; it is what permits us to see things and ourselves directly, impartially, without even passing through the medium of reason.

While the mind or reason are included in the soul (together with sentiment, memory, imagination, and will), the intel-

---

[3] See the chapter "What is the Intellect?", 45-50.

lect is "above" the soul (or, according to another perspective, in its deepest center, in the point that transcends the individual ego). The intellect is much more comprehensive than reason and thought, and involves the intuition of timeless realities, as Titus Burckhardt has noted.[4] The intellect, then, is what man possesses of a universal, objective, and perennial character.

According to Saint Thomas Aquinas, the intellect is the capacity of seeing things *sub specie aeternitatis*, that is, according to the "point of view of eternity". For Frithjof Schuon, what Revelation is for the macrocosm, the intellect is for the microcosm; what the divine Word represents for the exterior world, the intellect represents for the interior one. As he wrote, "the intellect . . . can know all that is knowable".[5]

In the striking words of Hermes Trismegistus, "it is by the light of the intellect that the human soul is illumined, as the world is illuminated by the Sun—no, in an even greater measure!"

In other words, the intellect transcends the psychic plane, it is not subject to the subjective coming and going; only the intellect can see through the ego's ambiguities, fluctuations, and uncertainties. As Titus Burckhardt has rightly observed, if everything is psychological, with what right does psychology present itself as the supreme instance of knowledge, given that it also fails to transcend the level of "psychic activity"?

JUNG: NEITHER *YIN* NOR *YANG*!

Jung showed an interest in Eastern culture, but this never went beyond a certain superficial acquaintance, and his mental horizons were always aligned with Western modernism and relativism. One can illustrate this fact by the way he "escaped" from a personal contact with the greatest saint of modern India, Sri Ramana Maharshi (1879-1950).

---

[4] *Mirror of the Intellect*, 219.
[5] *Sufism: Veil and Quintessence*, "Appendix", 136.

Jung visited India in 1937 and, having arranged a meeting with the Maharshi, at the last moment he alleged a futile reason for not going. As Jung wrote in his "The Holy Men of India",[6] "The fact is, I doubt his uniqueness; he is of a type that always was and will be. Therefore it was not necessary to seek him out. . . . The man who is only wise and only holy interests me about as much as the skeleton of a rare saurian, which would not move me to tears."

Besides, as the presumptuousness of the commentary denotes, the episode is revealing also in other aspects. Sri Ramana Maharshi was the representative *par excellence* of the spiritually "extinct" ego, purified and united with the Divine Self, being as he was the incarnation of those virtues which comprise the sage and the saint in all cultures: spiritual discernment, humility, generosity, total detachment to self.

Jung, for his part, did not, to say the least, possess such high qualities, and was not devoid of the desire for fame, wealth, and power. Notwithstanding this, he believed himself to be a model of "individuation" (more of this later). Narcissus finds only ugliness in what is not a mirror of himself, says popular wisdom. Jung avoided facing a man who had tamed the dragon of the ego and had no illusions about the world. Jung felt, as it were, intimidated by the spiritual power, which through such a meeting, would expose him. He turned his back on traditional spirituality in a reflex of self-defense, as he feared—"unconsciously", this is the right place to say so—the contact with a representative of traditional wisdom whose mere existence belied in actual practice his psychologizing theories.

The wisdom which the Maharshi expounded and lived, that of the non-dualist Vedanta, teaches that the world, and the ego which is a part of it, is relative or "illusory" in the last instance; only the Absolute is real. But, as a consequence

---

[6] *Psychology and Religion: West and East. Collected Works*, vol. XI, 577, 578.

of this highly metaphysical conception, it points out that the soul, in her most profound dimension, does not pertain to anything other than that of the real. In the elliptical terms of the Vedanta: "Brahma is real, the world is appearance; the soul's essence is not other than Brahma".

Jung, for his part, taught that each man must experience directly, without reference to traditional methods, his own "personal God" and should follow his "own law". The process of individuation would cause people to question their conventional religious, social, and moral supports. In "Adaptation, Individuation, Collectivity", Jung speaks as if he were a "prophet" of his "own" religion: "The individual must now consolidate himself by cutting himself off from God and becoming wholly himself."[7]

From this point of view, the soul needs no purification or purgation as an initial stage for spiritual advancement or fulfillment, nor any religious supports that lead towards this purification. The similarities between the two approaches— the traditional and the Jungian—are, to say the least, superficial and in fact deceptive. The first perspective indicates that the fallen soul is dominated by egoism and passion; it needs to be "tamed". It is the way of detachment, of the "extinction" of passions and egoism, which must become second nature. This is the first step of the spiritual path, only after which comes the phase of "union", in which the soul "enters" into the realm of the Real. Here the error of modern psychology is failure to take into account the need for the "cleansing" of the soul, that is, the eradication, or at least domination or control, of the vices, and the practice of the virtues. Jungian psychology, however, says nothing about this initial stage. The question at issue is as follows: is this not exactly the teaching of the symbolism of the "serpent" in the Garden of Eden, namely, that "man is God"? In fact, this was already claimed

[7]   *The Symbolic Life. Collected Works*, vol. XVIII, 453.

by heterodox Gnosticism during the early centuries of the Christian era; and it was Gnosticism that fascinated Jung.

Be that as it may, some see in Jungianism, when compared to Freudianism, a greater degree of similarity to traditional spiritualities. It is true that while Freud boasted of the fact that he was an irreconcilable enemy of religion, Jung claimed "sympathy" for it, while in reality emptying it of its deeper contents, which were replaced by the notion of collective psychism.

Jung tried, it is true, to bring psychology nearer to philosophy, but affirmed that the act of thinking, the foundation of philosophy, was, like everything else, no more than a psychical activity. This amounts to discarding objective truth and putting everything in the common ditch of the subjective.

A similar operation can be observed in the sense in which he used the term "archetype". Contrary to its normal and metaphysical meaning—the eternal ideas that are in the "mind of God" or in the divine intellect, perennial ideas that are beyond time and space, being essentially manifest in all civilizations under different forms—Jung considered the archetypes as "structures of the collective unconscious", and as part and parcel of the psychological dimension, without any intellectual and objective meaning.

As Harry Oldmeadow rightly observed,[8] one can see in Jung the tendency to repeatedly reduce metaphysics and religion to the psychic dimension alone, as if this latter should always have the last word. This tendency ended by contaminating all spheres of human activity, marking culture, history, art, and even religion, with its relativistic stamp. Under the slightest touch of Jungianism, everything becomes "psychological", that is, subjective and relative.

---

[8] See *Journeys East: 20th Century Western Encounters with Eastern Religious Traditions*, 317-323.

THE INFLUENCE OF SPIRITISM AND BREAKUP WITH FREUD

In the famous *Turm*, the tower Jung built in 1923 on his property on the banks of Lake Zurich, there was in his bedroom a great mural painting. It depicted a so called "Philemon", whom Jung considered to be his "guide" in the world of "spirits". It was through this being that Jung said he received "inspiration" for his concepts of the archetypes and the collective unconscious. The spiritist influence remained with him all his life and he participated in diverse paranormal sessions.

Jung met Freud in 1907; he immediately saw in psychoanalysis a religious potential, which he wanted to make converge with his great interest in the ancient German paganism. Concomitantly with this, he considered Christianity to be a development of Judaism and, therefore, a Semitic spirituality—something German peoples had to get rid of, turning instead to their own national roots even in the religious order. All these factors, including a strong link to spiritism, occultism, and what he considered to be ancient German paganism, contributed to the break with Freud in 1913.

From the point of view of psychology, Jung thought that Freud had exaggerated the role of sexuality and of repression in the psychic life, as well as of the importance of fantasies and traumas in childhood. He also criticized the dogmatism with which these theses were upheld. Jung saw Freud as a destroyer of tradition, as an iconoclast, but not as the "avatar" of a new age—an important role which Jung reserved for himself. In fact he regarded himself as a kind of "messenger" of a "new" religion, the religion of Jungianism, or the "cult of Jung".[9]

We have already seen in the preceding chapter, Freud's opinions about traditional religion, and it is not necessary to present them here again in detail; it is enough to remember that Freud considered the expression of anything spiritual to be a consequence of "repressed sexuality". He had a reduc-

---

[9] See in this respect Richard Noll, *The Jung Cult: Origins of a Charismatic Movement*.

tionist view of religion. To quote a critic of such opinions, let us cite the historian of religions Mircea Eliade, who rejected Freud's lucubration's about the topic:

> It is highly significant that such frantic hypotheses ["the horror stories presented as objective historical fact in *Totem and Taboo*"] could be acclaimed as sound scientific theory, in spite of all the criticism marshaled by the major anthropologists of the century. . . . After 1920, then, the Freudian ideology was taken for granted in its entirety. . . . Using the very tools and method of psychoanalysis, we can lay open some tragic secrets of the modern Western intellectual: for example, his profound dissatisfaction with the worn-out forms of historical Christianity and his desire to violently rid himself of his forefathers' faith, accompanied by a strange sense of guilt, as if he himself had killed a God in whom he could not believe but whose absence he could not bear.[10]

The Process of "Individuation"

For Jung, the collective unconscious is formed from the waste of primitive peoples' beliefs and it is to these beliefs and practices that people should turn in order to integrate their lives in the process of *individuation*—a kind of "liberation" in which the traditional contours and structures are replaced by who knows what.

Harry Oldmeadow made a pertinent evaluation of the topic in his book *Journeys East*, saying that he does not envisage Jung as a true sage, much less as a kind of "prophet", since he typifies some of the "confusions of the age in [his] life and work". On the more positive side, Jung was "profoundly concerned with man's position in a world in which science had stripped the cosmos of meaning, apparently eroded the

---

[10] *Occultism, Witchcraft, and Cultural Fashions: Essays in Comparative Religion*, 5.

pillars of religious faith, and robbed man of his spiritual dignity". Jung contributed, according to Oldmeadow, to a certain ransom of psychology and the study of religion from the claws of materialism, and also suggested bridges between religion and science, East and West. Nevertheless, if the question is to note whatever may be valid in his works, "one has to maintain a sense of proportion and apply a discernment which . . . can only be drawn from the treasuries of metaphysical and spiritual teachings found within the integral religious traditions."[11]

The Austro-American philosopher and scientist Wolfgang Smith has some tougher words on the topic:

> In the final analysis, what Jung has to offer is a religion for atheists and a mysticism for those who love only themselves. On the one hand, he extols what he terms the religious attitude as "an element in psychic life whose importance can hardly be overrated," while affirming, at the same time, that "the psychologist of today ought to realize once and for all that we are no longer dealing with questions of dogma and creed." In other words, it does not matter whether the objective content of religious belief is true or false: what counts is our subjective religious attitude, and presumably the sense of well-being which this is supposed to engender. . . . The "new product" is not like the old; it is an Ersatz . . . a religion for spiritual dilettantes who collect symbols and meanings as others collect paintings.[12]

To return to Oldmeadow, he concludes by pointing out that the crucial aspect towards which such evaluations point is the one many intellectuals prefer to ignore. Schuon has expounded it with clarity:

[11]   *Journeys East*, 123-124.
[12]   *Cosmos and Transcendence*, 130.

Outside tradition there can assuredly be found some relative truths or views of partial realities, but outside tradition there does not exist a doctrine that catalyzes absolute truth and transmits liberating notions concerning total Reality.[13]

BELIEVERS WITHOUT RELIGION

The Romanian philosopher Emil Cioran once referred to himself and to his friend Mircea Eliade in this way: "We would have been believers, but in fact we are all religious spirits without a religion".

I believe the same can be said about Jung. Here lies both his strength and his weakness. Strength because there is a certain cogency in his criticisms of a superficial religiosity, deprived of intelligence and conviction, lived conventionally, without the energy to penetrate deeply into consciences and hearts, and engaging all of man's being and thereby transforming him. But weakness because, without the integral spirituality that Jung rejected, a spirituality profoundly understood and lived in its highest dimensions, man loses his concrete bond with the sacred, a link which is provided by participation in the communal and individual religious practices, in other words, in the common rites and in solitary meditation and prayer, without forgetting the soul's conformity to a system of morality. Without such a bond, man loses his intellectual center and, in consequence, his spiritual and psychic balance.

---

[13] Frithjof Schuon, "No Activity without Truth", in *The Sword of Gnosis*, ed. Jacob Needleman, 36.

Chapter 10

Vatican II and the Three Revolutions

Corruptio optima pessima.
("The corruption of the best is the worst type of corruption.")
Latin Proverb

In the decades and centuries that followed the crucifixion of Christ, Christianity gradually took root and established itself as a world religion, especially in Europe and the Near East, but also in Africa and Asia. It reached its highpoint in what we now, retrospectively, call the Middle Ages—approximately from the coronation of Charlemagne in 800 AD to the thirteenth century.

It was in this epoch that the mystical orders such as the Franciscans and Dominicans flourished; schools of thought such as the Thomist (Aristotelian) and the Eckhartian (Platonic); artistic styles such as the Romanesque and the Gothic; sages and saints such as Francis of Assisi, Albertus Magnus, Bernard of Clairvaux, and Dante Alighieri. Not to mention the universities, hospitals, and other institutions the Church established.

Thereafter there have been three "revolutions", each of which greatly changed the face of Christendom. The first was the "Renaissance" (fifteenth century); the second the "Enlightenment" (eighteenth century); and the third and most catastrophic the Vatican II Council (twentieth century).

The Renaissance was the first fundamental movement away from "divinism" to "humanism", from *theocentrism* to *anthropocentrism*. The Enlightenment was a repetition of this, but in a much more arrogant and explicit way. The Vatican II Council (1962-1965) was the final and most devastating of the three revolutions because it overturned, from the inside as it were, traditional Catholic beliefs and practices. The Council thus reinforced, in an aggressive and destructive manner, and within the citadel of religion itself, the two earlier revolutions.

The name itself for what we are referring to as the "first" revolution is misleading, for it was a "death", not a "renaissance", of the medieval intellectual, spiritual, and cultural patrimony. This legacy includes centuries of theological speculation as expounded and synthesized in Saint Thomas Aquinas' *Summa*; Dante's *Divine Comedy*, comprising a vision and a teaching regarding man's posthumous destiny; the highly spiritual Romanesque and Gothic art and architecture; Byzantine icons, and many other things. The Renaissance was the first movement away from spirituality, transcendence, quality, inwardness, depth, and verticality, towards a new emphasis on materialism, worldliness, quantity, outwardness, superficiality, and horizontality. Not forgetting the substitution of universalism by individualism, of intellectuality by a rationalism (devoid of true premises), of Heaven by earth. In a word, the Renaissance meant the beginning of the "reign of quantity", such as was brilliantly explained by René Guénon in his books, especially in *The Crisis of the Modern World* (1927), and *The Reign of Quantity and the Sign of the Times* (1945).

Three centuries after the "Renaissance", a second revolution occurred which betrayed its true purpose by its very name; the leaders of the so-called "Enlightenment" saw themselves as bearers of the "light" of reason and science, as opposed to the "darkness" of "superstition" and "dogma". It was an ideological battle against religion. Characteristically, the movement was disseminated by a freemasonry which was already secularized and which served as an ideological basis for the French Revolution. The reduction of quality to quantity, of spirituality to materialism, of inwardness to outwardness experienced thus a second stage, and represented a radicalization which went far beyond the revolution that was the Renaissance.

The "reign of quantity" which had its first beginnings in the Renaissance, and its expansion in the Enlightenment, reached the citadel of religion itself with the Vatican II Council of 1962-1965. In the council one saw the new humanist ideology of science, "progress", and technology invading the sacred precincts once reserved for the knowledge and love of God. But since religion is in no way a support for the materialistic mentality as promulgated by the Renaissance and the Enlightenment—and indeed is in direct opposition to it—the leaders of the council sought above all to achieve a "pact" and an accommodation with modernity. This aim is a direct betrayal of the Christian spirit. As René Guénon observed in *The Crisis of the Modern World* (written in the 1927, long before Vatican II), "there can be nothing but antagonism between the religious spirit, in the true sense of the word, and the modern mentality, and any compromise is bound to weaken the former and favor the latter, whose hostility moreover will not be placated thereby, since it can only aim at the utter destruction of everything that reflects in mankind a reality higher than the human."[1] Prophetic words.[2]

The principal architect of this revolution inside the Catholic Church was the French Jesuit Teilhard de Chardin; he was the "missing link" (!) between the Renaissance and the Enlightenment, on the one hand, and Vatican II, on the other hand. Together with Teilhard, we could say that our epoch is dominated by the specters of Darwin, Marx, Freud, and Jung. One may consider their influence to be something of the past, but they have left deep and lasting impressions on our ways of thinking and doing. In a certain sense, they remain the essential components of the received "religion" of today, being in fact the roots of our secular "religion". This (pseudo-) reli-

---

[1] *The Crisis of the Modern World*, 95.

[2] It is worth remembering that, according to the Gospels themselves, St. Peter denied Christ three times. Symbolically it can be said that the church Peter established "inherited", so to speak, these refusals, and they can be identified as the three great denials we are speaking of.

gion also has its "fundamentalist" defenders, who manifest a "religious intolerance" that surpasses even the worst examples of the past. What people refer to as the "religious bigotry" of past ages has been outdone—by far—by the bigotry of the "religion" of the present age. Anyone who calls these modern beliefs in question runs a serious risk![3]

Very few institutions have not been touched by the ideas associated with these names. They are ubiquitous, and they show themselves, in different ways and to different degrees, in many and varied domains. Because of its importance in the Western world, it is worth considering how and to what extent these trends have affected the Catholic Church. In fact, they have done so in the shape of the revolution that was the Vatican II Council. Apart from the general influences of Darwin and Marx, one can say that the behind-the-scenes architect of this council was the "ghost" of the already deceased Teilhard de Chardin (1881-1955). This French Jesuit became known for proposing a kind of evolutionistic pantheism with a Christian veneer. Among other things, Teilhard used to teach that Christ represented an "evolutionary leap" of great magnitude. His "testament" can be summarized by a piece from his book, *Christianity and Evolution*:

> If as a result of some interior revolution, I were to lose in succession my faith in Christ, my faith in a personal God, and my faith in spirit, I feel that I should continue to believe invincibly in the world. The world (its value, its infallibility, and its goodness)—that, when all is said and done, is the first, the last, and the only thing in which I believe.

It is not for nothing that someone justly said that while Luther was a Christian who left the Catholic Church, Teilhard was a pagan who remained in it!

---

[3]   See, in this respect, William Stoddart, *Invincible Wisdom*, 97.

The nature of the Vatican II revolution is most clearly revealed in the declarations of the five post-Vatican-II popes themselves. But before proceeding with these declarations, let us explain that Vatican II is viewed in this book as an extended expression of the concept of "secular fundamentalism". Its main ideologue, the just-quoted Teilhard de Chardin, was a kind of continuator of Marx and Darwin from within the Catholic Church, and one of the leaders of Catholic modernism. The ideology of Vatican II may thus be considered as a "fundamentalism" of the modernistic kind, an expression of the belief that everything modern is better than anything ancient. Vatican II is "fundamentalist" in its emotional and prejudiced attachment to modernistic ideas, despising the millennial tradition of age-old Christianity; it is "fundamentalistically" opposed to the true spirit of Christianity, and harmful to it; it is "fundamentalistically" superficial, non-traditional, and biased in its opposition to authentic spirituality.

Even with a program as radical and as unprecedented as Vatican II, it has given rise to little concern on the part of a passive public. The immensity of the break with tradition brought about by the council is not widely appreciated. The quotations below from Giovanni Battista Montini, the second of the five post-Vatican-II popes, indicate all too clearly how drastic the revolution was. His words are in direct opposition to Christianity in its very foundations.

PAUL VI (REIGNED 1963-1978)

At his general audience on 2nd July 1969, Paul VI, with an exceptional clarity, declared: "One cannot avoid making the spontaneous reflection: 'If the whole world is changing, should not religion change also?'"

Opening the fourth session [of the Vatican II Council] on 14th September 1965, he stated to the whole assembly: "The Council offers the Church . . . a panoramic vision of the world. Can the Church, and can we ourselves, do anything other than to look upon the world and love it?"

But it is in his closing speech [at the Council] on 7th December 1965 that we find the core of the matter: "A current of love and admiration has overflowed from the Council onto the modern human world. . . . Its values have not only been respected, but honored; its efforts have been approved, its aspirations purified and blessed."

At his audience of 5th March 1969, Paul VI confided: "How does the Church look upon the world of today? The way the Church looks upon the world has been enlarged so as to modify appreciably the attitude that we have towards it. The doctrine of the Church has been enriched by a more complete knowledge of its nature and its mission. . . . This presupposes a different mentality, a mentality we can describe as new."

Paul VI, with a particular eloquence, enthused at the most solemn moment of the Council, and I extract these passages from his closing speech on 7th December 1965: "All the doctrinal richness of the Council has but one aim: to serve man. . . . All things considered, does not the Council deliver a simple, new, and solemn lesson by teaching that we must love man in order to love God? . . . To know God, it is necessary to know man! . . . The discovery of human needs—and they are all the greater because the son of the earth has become greater!—has absorbed the attention of this synod. Recognize in it, you modern humanists who renounce the transcendence of supreme things, at least this merit, and know how to recognize our new humanism: We too, We more than anyone, We have the Cult of Man."[4]

---

[4]   Paul VI, quoted in Hubert Montheilhet, *Paul VI*, 65-66.

BENEDICT XVI (REIGN 2005-PRESENT)

As regards Joseph Ratzinger, the fifth of the five post-Vatican-II popes, the following quotations reveal only too clearly the extent to which the traditional Catholic Church has been destroyed. He is still, but wrongly, called a "conservative"—and this since the beginning of his ecclesiastical career. Already in the 1950s, his habilitation thesis at the Freising seminar in Germany was refused by the then Church's "pre-revolutionary" authorities, because of "lack of theological rigor", "suspicion of neo-modernist heterodoxy", and also for "subjectivizing the concept of Revelation". In his autobiography *La Mia Vita*, he criticized the principal theological school of Catholicism, namely Thomism, for being "closed in on itself, impersonal, and pre-fabricated".

The true ideology of Benedict XVI can therefore be best understood simply by paying attention to his own words. In *Principles of Catholic Theology*, he praises the "impulse given by Teilhard de Chardin", whose "bold vision incorporated the historical movement of Christianity into the evolutionary process".

In the same book, he wrote that "Truth becomes a function of time. . . . Fidelity to yesterday's truth consists precisely in abandoning it in assuming it into today's truth." The same author, nevertheless, described the "dictatorship of relativism" as the "central problem of our faith today" (in the Mass *Pro eligendo pontifice*, one day before he was elected by the cardinals). But the core of relativism is the idea that nothing is definitive, and that truth is dependent on history. In this connection, Aristotle said: "Those who declare that everything, including the truth, follows a constant flux, contradict themselves, for, if everything changes, on which basis can they formulate a valid statement?"

This "neo-modernist" theology is widespread also among the close helpers of Benedict XVI. To give one example, he brought to Rome, as the prefect of the Congregation for the Clergy, the Brazilian cardinal Cláudio Hummes. In an interview for the Brazilian newspaper *Folha de São Paulo* (5 November 2006), just before embarking for the Vatican at the end of 2006, he supported the "evolution of the dogmas". According to Catholic theology, the dogmas are divinely revealed truths, therefore immutable; they are the pillars upon which the edifice of the religion is built; without them, or with them in mutation, or in "evolution", what would guarantee the stability and permanency of the religious building? Pope Saint Pius X (Giuseppe Melchiorre Sarto, 1835-1914) wrote in the encyclical *Pascendi*: "If anyone says that the dogmas evolve, let him be anathema."

In his lecture at the Convent of Saint Scholastica, in Subiaco, Italy (1st April 2005), Ratzinger said: "The Enlightenment is of Christian origin and it is no accident that it was born precisely and exclusively in the realm of the Christian faith... . It was the merit of the Enlightenment that it proposed anew these original values of Christianity. . . . In the pastoral constitution 'On the Church in the Modern World', Vatican Council II once again underlined this profound correspondence between Christianity and the Enlightenment, seeking to come to a true conciliation between the Church and modernity."

The paradox of the head of the new church claiming the "glory" of the Enlightenment for Christianity is that this eighteenth century movement, as we have said, was marked by a strong anti-religious sentiment. This is attested by the "wish" made by one of the leaders of the Enlightenment, Denis Diderot (1713-1784), who looked forward to a world where "the last King would be hanged in the entrails of the last Pope". Let us only hope that the "profound correspondence" does not go so far!

Compared with his immediate predecessors, Benedict XVI opened a new phase in the recent history of the Church, and inaugurated a new "concept" of *pontifex*. The simple choice of his name means something significant. The signal he sent is that he is not a John Paul III, nor simply one more John or Paul, much less a Pius, whose name would indicate an anti-modernistic approach, for it was pope Pius X (1903-1914) who defined modernism as the "synthesis of all heresies". Ratzinger admitted that his "point of reference" is Benedict XV (1914-1922), a conciliatory pope who reigned during the First World War. Therefore, what Benedict XVI seeks to do is "conciliate"; to conciliate, if this were possible, revolution with tradition. In fact, his actions point in the direction of a correction of "excesses". At the same time, he seeks an *entente* between contraries, from which stems the whole ambiguity of his approach.

He informs us that while he was a radical leftist theologian during the Second Vatican Council, he is now considered a "conservative". His eminence has admitted, however, that he has not moved to the right in four decades, but that the world has moved so far to the left that even a progressive of his conviction looks traditional.[5]

"By their fruits ye shall know them": this fundamental teaching of Christ is the key for understanding the current situation. In fact, since the end of the council in the 1960s, thousands of priests have abandoned the priesthood; according to *Civiltá Cattolica* (21st April 2007), the number of ex-priests between 1964 and 2004 reaches 69,063.

Vocations are scarce in the secular clergy as well as in the religious orders such as the Benedictines, Franciscans, Dominicans, and Jesuits. All over the world, seminars, schools, and convents have been closed. In the United States, from the 49,000 seminarians functioning in 1965, there are only 4,700 today. The number of nuns has dropped from 180,000 in 1965, to 75,000 in 2002. There were 1,566 Catholic schools in the USA in 1965; now there are 786. The students in those schools dropped from 700,000 to 386,000 in the same period. Attendance at Sunday Mass has fallen to less than 20% of the faithful, although it was 75% in the 1960s. In Brazil, "the lar-

---

[5] *Washington Times*, 30 September 2003. Quoted by Rama Coomaraswamy in *The Destruction of the Christian Tradition*, 437.

gest Catholic country in the world", with more than 100 million faithful, the Church has been losing almost a million souls a year during the last three decades. From the 1960s until now, the number of Catholics has dropped from 90% of the total population to 73%, and continues to drop further. In the same period, the number of atheists and agnostics greatly increased, from 0.5% to 7.4% of the total population. In Western Europe almost half of newborn infants are no longer baptized.

It is worth noting that the Eastern Churches, on the other hand, which have not modified their beliefs and rites, are faring relatively well—and the Catholic churches of the Oriental rite, such as the Melkite, the Ukrainian, the Armenian, etc., do not face a crisis as intense as do their Roman counterpart. On the contrary, they receive many recruits from the Roman Church, who are considered "refugees from Vatican II"!

All things considered, the core of the matter is that Benedict XVI now reaps the perverse and distant effects of the revolution he helped to foment in the past. Now he seeks to control, limit, or abolish—depending on the case—the destructive consequences of the transformations he once stimulated in the past. But he limits himself to the effects. He takes aim at the "excesses", not the roots of what he himself once called the Church's "self-demolition" following Vatican II. His agenda, then, points in the direction of a contradictory "convergence" or *entente* between Catholic modernism and tradition, towards an impossible "consonance" between irreconcilable opponents. Can he be successful in this Herculean task? Or will he simply engage in a work of Sisyphus?[6]

---

[6] I am indebted to Rama Coomaraswamy, *The Destruction of the Christian Tradition*, 436-437 for the quotations from Benedict XVI. Above all, I am grateful to William Stoddart for the insights provided in his two recent books, *What Do the Religions say about Each Other?* and *Invincible Wisdom*.

Chapter 11

Science Fundamentalism: A Short Answer to Three Militant Atheists

It is not their eyes that are blind, but their hearts.

Koran 22:46

They reckon ill who leave Me [God] out.

Ralph Waldo Emerson (in his poem "Brahma")

Secular or atheistic fundamentalism is a reaction *par en bas* against religious fundamentalism; it is a new form of superficiality and intolerance advanced by a few anti-religious polemicists. Ideas have consequences: this is the first thing an intellectual should know. But this does not seem to be the case for men such as Richard Dawkins, Christopher Hitchens, or Samuel Harris.

These authors, pushing the limits of science beyond its boundaries, openly defend the "eradication" of the religious traditions of humanity. In a sense, they are only resorting to an old human instinct of blaming this or that set of ideas or groups for all the miseries of the world; this was done with the Chinese, the Germans, the Russians, the Jews, the Arabs, the religious, the makers of pizza, etc. For these superficial and inconsequential critics, it is as if it is enough to get rid of religion for the world to be a perfect paradise. The least one can say is that in the past, this kind of action did not produce good fruits! Far from it! It is a case, not of "ethnic cleansing"—now widespread throughout the world—but of "religious cleansing". In the opinion of this trio of destroyers, the religions have not brought anything positive to humanity; they are marked by intellectual insufficiency. Besides, according to them, they are a "risk" for our very existence.

Nothing positive? What to say then of Chartres cathedral, the Taj Mahal, the Alhambra, and the pinnacles of Buddhist sculpture? What to say of the time-honored wisdom of Lao Tzu, Shankara, St. Augustine, and Ibn Arabi? All these "monuments", intellectual and architectural, are in fact direct manifestations of a religious spirit that has never ceased to exist among all peoples. One should also remember that the positive presence of religion extends even to the more prosaic and mundane aspects of our life, such as the culture of wine and ale—which owes its present diffusion and sophistication to the work implemented in Europe by monks back in the Middle Ages. Nor must one forget the universities, the Sorbonne for instance, and the hospitals created and maintained by the Church; nor the cities which owe all their charm to the Spirit: Istanbul, Fez, Cairo, Varanasi, Kyoto, Jerusalem, Ravenna, Venice, Siena, Toledo, Ávila, and many others.

Intellectual frailty? In their "scientistic crusade" have these righteous of the lab coat never heard of the *Bhagavad Gītā*, the *Tao Te Ching*, the *Dhammapada* of the Buddha, or the Sermon on the Mount? Do Dante and the *Divine Comedy* mean nothing to the new inquisitors of secular fundamentalism?

Irrationality? How then do they explain the genius of Pascal, Ralph Waldo Emerson, and Padre Vieira?[1] What about

---

[1] Padre Vieira, a Luso-Brazilian master of medieval intellectuality, was born in Lisbon, Portugal, in 1608. He arrived in Brazil at seven years of age, in 1615. In the city of Salvador, Bahia, Vieira received his early education and later made his vows, being ordained as a priest in the Society of Jesus. Brazil was his adopted country and there he combated the Inquisition, as well as the Dutch attacks; he defended the Indians and the Negroes against slavery, and the Jews against forced conversion. For these positions he acquired many enemies, being imprisoned more than once. He died in Salvador in 1697 at the age of 89. His works include *History of the Future*, *The Art of Dying*, *On Prophecy and Inquisition*, as well as hundreds of magnificent sermons and thousands of letters.

Shakespeare, Cervantes, Calderón, Rumi, and Guimarães Rosa.[2] Is the supreme music of Bach, Mozart, and the Gregorian chant, a "risk" for our survival? And what of the ethereal Red Indian Sun Dance and the ecstatic whirl of the Sufi dervishes? Solomon was right when he said, some three thousand years ago, that there is nothing new under the sun. These polemicists believe they are propounding something original, but they do not say anything essentially different from the atheists of Greece, India, and other places of antiquity. They repeat the discourse of the Sophists of 2,500 years ago. Freud and Marx also tried to "eradicate" religion with the stroke of a pen. All of them forget that there has never been a civilization, throughout human history, without a religion. "There is no culture without cult", as T.S. Eliot said. The only element of "innovation" in the current movement of Dawkins, Hitchens, Harris, et al., is the typically "modern" lack of imagination and arrogance.

These authors, moreover, exceed the proper field of science, and in practice turn it into a (pseudo-) religion; their anti-religion becomes a "new religion", much more intolerant than the ones it means to fight.

"When the finger points at the moon, the foolish man looks at the finger", says a Zen proverb. What a world without salt and charm is the one that Dawkins and comrades envisage! A world without the wisdom of Confucius, the spiritual presence and example of the saints, the temples and music of India; a world without perfume, without beauty, without virtue; even more importantly, a life without meaning and purpose. These men have spent too much time in a laboratory and have not perceived that much of the good we still

---

[2] Guimarães Rosa (1908-1967) is the greatest writer in Brazil, author of the novel *Grande Sertão: Veredas* (translated as "The Devil to Pay in the Backlands"), which some consider as a contemporary successor to Dante's *Divine Comedy* and Homer's *Odyssey*.

have derives from the wisdom transmitted by religion. Not "religion" superficially and fanatically understood, of course, but the religion of the True, the Good, and the Beautiful about which Plato, among others, spoke.

Corruptio optimi pessima: the corruption of the best is the worst type of corruption. Politically, this adage can be applied to the so-called "religious right", with its grave errors, its narcissism, and its self-indulgence. But the polemicists we have in view are not primarily criticizing the religious right; they are proposing the wholesale destruction of religion.

Finally, one has to respond to their pseudo-arguments by pointing out that the great disgraces of the twentieth century were not caused by religion. Neither the First nor the Second World War had anything to do with religion; Nazism and Communism were strongly anti-religious, persecuting every kind of believer. The United States president Harry Truman gave his approval to the dropping of atomic bombs upon Hiroshima and Nagasaki; nothing to do with any religion here. On the contrary, it was the fundamentalists of science and technology that produced these bombs and the unprincipled and immoral politicians that launched them.

In short, these anti-religious opportunists hide the fact that none of our recent tragedies had a religious motivation, apart, of course, from the militant religious fundamentalists. The "intelligent bombs" and the "surgical attacks" were fabricated by Dawkins' comrades. Modern dictatorships—"rational", "scientific", and violently anti-religious—persecuted and killed thousands of Christians, Muslims, and Jews in the epoch of the Soviet Union and Nazism, and millions of Buddhists and Taoists were killed in the "Cultural Revolution" of Mao Tse Tung's China. The worst kings and sultans of history were like noisy little boys when compared with these leaders of mass destruction

Did Jesus, Buddha, and Muhammad, all founders of world religions, not know what they were doing? Is this faction of science fundamentalists wiser than they? Human perversion and depravation is enough to explain our miseries, as Schuon and his followers,[3] have explained in their magnificent books. And if religions are not totally innocent—remember that Christ said, "Why callest thou Me good? There is none good but God"—it is nevertheless thanks to religion and its manifold examples of wisdom and love, that the good does not vanish from the face of the earth.

[3]   See especially William Stoddart, *Remembering in a World of Forgetting*, "Frithjof Schuon and the Perennialist School".

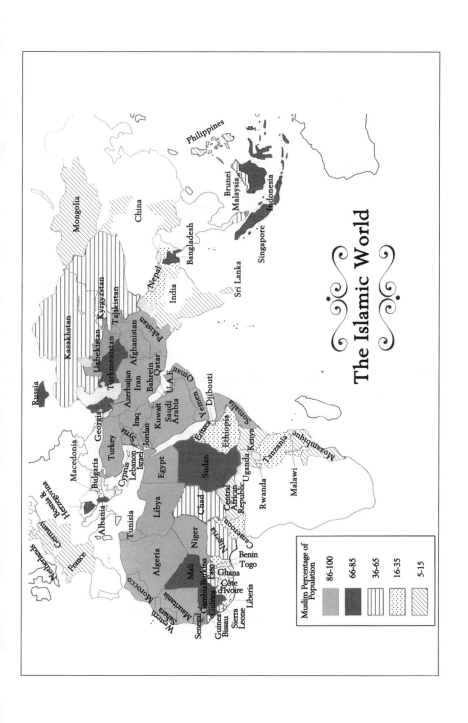

The Islamic World

Muslim Percentage of Population
- 86-100
- 66-85
- 36-65
- 16-35
- 5-15

SELECTED BIBLIOGRAPHY

Armstrong, Karen. *The Battle for God: Fundamentalism in Judaism, Christianity, and Islam*. New York: Harper Collins, 2001.

Bakan, David. *Freud and the Jewish Mystical Tradition*. New York: Dover, 2004.

Burckhardt, Titus. *Mirror of the Intellect: Essays on Traditional Science and Sacred Art*. Cambridge, UK: Quinta Essentia, 1987.

————. *Fez: City of Islam*. Cambridge, UK: Islamic Texts Society, 1992.

————. *Moorish Culture in Spain*. Louisville, KY: Fons Vitae, 1999.

————. *Sacred Art in East and West*. Louisville, KY/ Bloomington, IN: Fons Vitae/World Wisdom, 2001.

————. *The Essential Titus Burckhardt: Reflections on Sacred Art, Faiths, and Civilizations*. Bloomington, IN: World Wisdom, 2003.

————. *An Introduction to Sufi Doctrine*. Bloomington, IN: World Wisdom, 2006.

————. *Siena: City of the Virgin*. Bloomington, IN: World Wisdom, 2006.

Chodkiewicz, Michel. *The Spiritual Writings of Amir 'Abd al-Kader*. Albany, NY: SUNY Press, 1995.

Coomaraswamy, Rama P. *The Destruction of the Christian Tradition*. Bloomington, IN: World Wisdom, 2006.

Danner, Victor. "The Last Days in Judaism, Christianity, and Islam". In *Fragments of Infinity: Essays in Religion and Philosophy*, edited by Arvind Sharma. New York: Avery Publishing Group, 1991.

Eliade, Mircea. *No Souvenirs*. New York: Harper & Row, 1977.

————. *Occultism, Witchcraft, and Cultural Fashions: Essays in Comparative Religion*. Chicago: Chicago University

Press, 1976.

Faingold, Reuven. *Dom Pedro na Terra Santa*. São Paulo: Sêfer, 1999.

Finkelstein, Norman. *The Holocaust Industry*. New York: Verso, 2003.

Fitzgerald, Michael Oren & Judith Fitzgerald. *The Universal Spirit of Islam*. Bloomington, IN: World Wisdom, 2007.

Freud, Sigmund. *Totem and Taboo*. New York: W.W Norton and Co., 1989.

————. *The Future of an Illusion*. New York: W.W Norton and Co., 1989.

————. *Moses and Monotheism*. London: Hogarth Press, 1975.

————. *Outline of Psychoanalysis*. New York: W.W Norton and Co., 1989.

Garaudy, Roger. *The Founding Myths of Modern Israel*. Newport Beach, CA: Institute for Historical Review, 2000.

Geoffroy, Éric. *Introduction to Sufism: The Inner Path of Islam*. Bloomington, IN: World Wisdom, 2010.

Guénon, René. *The Crisis of the Modern World*. Hillsdale, NY: Sophia Perennis, 2001.

————. *The Reign of Quantity and the Signs of the Times*. Hillsdale, NY: Sophia Perennis, 2002.

————. *Insights into Islamic Esoterism and Taoism*. Hillsdale, NY: Sophia Perennis, 2003.

Guerriero, Silas (ed.). *O estudo das religiões: desafios contemporâneos*. São Paulo: Paulinas, 2003.

Ibn Khaldun. *Muqaddimah: An Introduction to History*. Princeton, NJ: Princeton University Press, 2004.

Jung, Carl G. *Psychology and Religion: West and East. Collected Works of C.G. Jung, Vol. XI*. Princeton, NJ: Princeton University Press, 1975.

————. *The Symbolic Life. Collected Works of C.G. Jung, Vol. XVIII*. Princeton, NJ: Princeton University Press, 1977.

Khalidi, Tarif. *The Muslim Jesus: Sayings and Stories in Islamic*

Literature. Cambridge, MA: Harvard University Press, 2003.

Lamartine, Alphonse. *History of Turkey (1857).* General Books, 2009.

Lindbom, Tage. *The Myth of Democracy.* Grand Rapids, MI: William B. Eerdmans, 1996.

Lings, Martin. *Muhammad : His Life Based on the Earliest Sources.* Cambridge, UK: Islamic Texts Society, 1983.

———. *A Sufi Saint of the Twentieth Century: Shaikh Ahmad al-ʿAlawī, His Spiritual Heritage and Legacy.* Cambridge, UK: Islamic Texts Society, 1993.

———. *What is Sufism?* Cambridge, UK: Islamic Texts Society, 1999.

———. *Ancient Beliefs and Modern Superstitions.* Cambridge, UK: Archetype, 2001.

———. *The Eleventh Hour: The Spiritual Crisis of the Modern World in the Light of Tradition and Prophecy.* Cambridge, UK: Archetype, 2002.

———. *A Return to the Spirit: Questions and Answers.* Louisville, KY: Fons Vitae, 2005.

———. *Symbol & Archetype: A Study of the Meaning of Existence.* Louisville, KY: Fons Vitae, 2006.

——— & Clinton Minnaar (eds.). *The Underlying Religion: An Introduction to the Perennial Philosophy.* Bloomington, IN: World Wisdom, 2007.

Lumbard, Joseph (ed.). *Islam, Fundamentalism, and the Betrayal of Tradition: Revised.* Bloomington, IN: World Wisdom, 2009.

Mearsheimer, John J. & Stephen M. Walt. *The Israel Lobby and US Foreign Policy.* New York: Farrar, Straus and Giroux, 2007.

Hubert Montheilhet. *Paul VI.* Paris: Nos Grands Hommes, 1978.

Nasr, Seyyed Hossein (ed.). *Islamic Spirituality I: Foundations.* New York: Crossroad, 1997.

———. *Islamic Spirituality II: Manifestations.* New York:

Crossroad, 1997.

Needleman, Jacob (ed.). *The Sword of Gnosis*. Baltimore: Penguin Books, 1974.

Noll, Richard. *The Jung Cult: Origins of a Charismatic Movement*. Chicago: Touchstone, 1997.

Oldmeadow, Harry. *Journeys East*. Bloomington, IN: World Wisdom, 2004.

Pappe, Ilan. *The Ethnic Cleansing of Palestine*. Oxford: Oneworld, 2007.

Perry, Whitall N. *Challenges to a Secular Society*. Oakton, VA: Foundation for Traditional Studies, 1996.

Pickthall, Mohammad Marmaduke (trans.). *The Meaning of the Glorious Koran*. Delhi: Taj Company, 1988.

Scholem, Gershom. "The Name of God and the Linguistic Theory of the Kabbalah". *Diogenes* 79 (Fall 1972): 59-80, and 80 (Winter 1972): 164-194.

Schuon, Frithjof. *Esoterism as Principle and as Way*. London: Perennial Books, 1981.

———. *Castes and Races*. London: Perennial Books, 1982.

———. *Survey of Metaphysics and Esoterism*. Bloomington, IN: World Wisdom, 1986.

———. *To Have a Center*. Bloomington, IN: World Wisdom, 1990.

———. *The Transcendent Unity of Religions*. Wheaton, IL: Quest, 1993.

———. *The Transfiguration of Man*. Bloomington, IN: World Wisdom, 1995.

———. *Understanding Islam*. Bloomington, IN: World Wisdom, 1998.

———. *Form and Substance in the Religions*. Bloomington, IN: World Wisdom, 2002.

———. *Light on the Ancient Worlds*. Bloomington, IN: World Wisdom, 2006.

———. *Sufism: Veil and Quintessence*. Bloomington, IN: World Wisdom, 2007.

———. *Christianity/Islam: Perspectives on Esoteric Ecumenism*. Bloomington, IN: World Wisdom, 2008.

————. *Logic and Transcendence.* Bloomington, IN: World Wisdom, 2009.

Smith, Wolfgang. *Cosmos and Transcendence.* La Salle, IL: Sherwood & Sugden, 1984.

————. *Teilhardism and the New Religion.* Rockford, IL: TAN, 1988.

Soares de Azevedo, Mateus. *Iniciação ao Islã e Sufismo.* Rio de Janeiro: Record, 2000.

————. *Mística islâmica.* Petrópolis: Vozes, 2001.

———— (ed.). *Ye Shall Know the Truth: Christianity and the Perennial Philosophy.* Bloomington, IN: World Wisdom, 2005.

————. *Inteligência da Fé: Cristianismo, Islã, Judaísmo.* Rio de Janeiro: Nova Era, 2006.

Stoddart, William. *Sufism: The Mystical Doctrines and Methods of Islam.* New York: Paragon House, 1986.

————. *Outline of Buddhism.* Washington DC: Foundation of Traditional Studies, 1998.

————. *Remembering in a World of Forgetting: Thoughts on Tradition and Postmodernism.* Bloomington, IN: World Wisdom, 2008.

————. *What Do the Religions say about Each Other? Christian Attitudes towards Islam, Islamic Attitudes towards Christianity.* San Raphael, CA: Sophia Perennis, 2008.

————. *Invincible Wisdom: Quotations from the Scriptures, Saints, and Sages of All Times and Places.* San Raphael, CA: Sophia Perennis, 2008.

Suhrawardy, Abdallah al-. *The Sayings of Muhammad.* New York: Citadel, 1995.

Wittels, Fritz. *Sigmund Freud: His Personality, His Teaching, and His School.* London: Allen & Unwin, 1924.

INDEX

Abd al-Qadir, Emir, 9-10
Absolute, 45, 65, 73, 85
ahādīth. See *hadīth*
al-Alawi, Shaykh, 32, 56, 57
Allāhu akbar, 44
Aristotle, 5, 26, 48, 99
Armstrong, Karen, 7, 111
Ataturk (Mustafa Kemal), 18, 32, 54
Augustine, St., 23, 29, 104

Benedict XVI (Joseph Ratzinger), 99, 100, 101, 102
Bhagavad Gītā, 10, 104
Bible, 11, 12, 13, 31, 34, 35
bin Laden, Osama, 6, 7, 52
Buddha, 27, 28, 60, 104, 106
Burckhardt, Titus, 60, 75, 76, 77, 84, 111, 117

Caesar, 15, 16, 36
Catholicism, 15, 29, 44, 72, 75, 99
Christ. See Jesus Christ
communism, 15
culture, 3, 8, 52, 59, 60, 67, 70, 84, 87, 104, 105

Darwin, Charles, 13, 95, 96, 97
Dawkins, Richard, 5, 103
dhikr, 44, 45, 46, 57, 59
Divine Comedy, 4, 94, 104, 105
Divine Name, the, 44, 57
Divinity, 24, 26, 73
dogmas, 65, 100

ego, 5, 9, 20, 34, 37, 84, 85
Eliade, Mircea, 77, 89, 91, 111
Enlightenment, the, 93, 94, 95, 100
esoterism,19, 25, 26, 39, 59, 61

Freud, Sigmund, 67, 68, 69, 70, 71, 72, 73, 74, 75, 77, 78, 81, 87, 88, 89, 95, 105, 111, 112, 115
Freudianism, 67, 74, 77, 78, 87

globalization, 6, 20
Gnosticism, 87
Gospels, the, 5, 35, 38, 95
Guénon, René, 25, 74, 77, 94, 95, 112

hadīth, 4, 39, 46
Harris, Samuel, 5, 103
heterodoxy, 7, 69, 99
Hitchens, Christopher, 5, 103

Ibn Arabi, 10, 19, 32, 58, 59, 104
individuation, 85, 86, 89
intellect, the, 83, 84, 87
Islamic esoterism, 25, 59. *See also* Sufism
Israel, 12, 19, 52, 112, 113

Jerusalem, 11, 12, 39, 46, 69, 71, 104
Jesus Christ, 4, 12, 14, 24, 29, 30, 32, 33, 35, 38, 41, 44, 75,

Index

For a glossary of all key foreign words used in books published by World Wisdom, including metaphysical terms in English, consult: www.DictionaryofSpiritualTerms.org.

This on-line Dictionary of Spiritual Terms provides extensive definitions, examples, and related terms in other languages.

BIOGRAPHICAL NOTES

MATEUS SOARES DE AZEVEDO is a writer and journalist from Minas Gerais, central Brazil. He studied journalism at the Catholic University of São Paulo, modern languages at the University of São Paulo, and History of Religions and International Relations at George Washington University (USA). He also holds a master's degree in the History of Religions from the University of São Paulo, with a thesis on the relevance of the Perennial Philosophy for contemporary thought. For many years he worked as a journalist in the International Affairs section of major newspapers.

He is the author of six books and more than 50 articles and essays on the importance of traditional religion and spirituality in the contemporary world, several of them translated into English and Spanish. He has contributed articles to journals and magazines in the USA, Canada, Spain, France, and Brazil, including the Perennialist journals *Sacred Web* and *Sophia*. He has also translated, and arranged for publication, books by C. S. Lewis, Frithjof Schuon, Martin Lings, and Rama Coomaraswamy in Portuguese. He is the editor of the anthology *Ye Shall Know The Truth: Christianity and the Perennial Philosophy* (World Wisdom, 2005). He lives with his wife and two children in São Paulo.

WILLIAM STODDART was born in Carstairs, Scotland, lived most of his life in London, England, and now lives in Windsor, Ontario. He studied modern languages, and later medicine, at the universities of Glasgow, Edinburgh, and Dublin. He was a close associate of both Frithjof Schuon and Titus Burckhardt during the lives of these leading Perennialists and translated several of their works into English. For many years Stoddart was assistant editor of the British journal *Studies in Comparative Religion*. Pursuing his interests in comparative religion, he has traveled widely in Europe, North Africa, India, Ceylon, and Japan. Stoddart's works include *Sufism: The Mystical Doctrines and Methods of*

Islam (1976), *Outline of Hinduism* (1993), *Outline of Buddhism* (1998), *Invincible Wisdom: Quotations from the Scriptures, Saints, and Sages of All Times and Places* (2008), and *What Do the Religions Say About Each Other?* (2008). His essential writings were recently published by World Wisdom as *Remembering in a World of Forgetting: Thoughts on Tradition and Postmodernism* (2008).

ALBERTO VASCONCELLOS QUEIROZ was born and raised in the Brazilian city of Santos, the largest seaport in Latin America. He studied psychology at the Pontifical Catholic University in São Paulo where he graduated as a professional psychologist. After graduating, he moved to the city of São José dos Campos, where he began his career working in industry. He soon turned to the public sector, initially as a psychologist in residential care units, and later as a municipal administrator. He is now an assistant to the Mayor's Office, with special responsibility for educational projects. He lives with his wife and six children in a beautiful country location not far from São José dos Campos.

Other Titles in the Perennial Philosophy Series by World Wisdom

The Betrayal of Tradition:
Essays on the Spiritual Crisis of Modernity,
edited by Harry Oldmeadow, 2005

Borderlands of the Spirit: Reflections on a Sacred Science of Mind,
by John Herlihy, 2005

A Buddhist Spectrum: Contributions to
Buddhist-Christian Dialogue, by Marco Pallis, 2003

A Christian Pilgrim in India: The Spiritual Journey of
Swami Abhishiktananda (Henri Le Saux),
by Harry Oldmeadow, 2008

The Essential Ananda K. Coomaraswamy,
edited by Rama P. Coomaraswamy, 2004

The Essential Martin Lings,
edited by Reza Shah-Kazemi and Emma Clark, 2011

The Essential René Guénon, edited by John Herlihy, 2009

The Essential Seyyed Hossein Nasr,
edited by William C. Chittick, 2007

The Essential Sophia,
edited by Seyyed Hossein Nasr and Katherine O'Brien, 2006

The Essential Titus Burckhardt: Reflections on Sacred Art, Faiths,
and Civilizations, edited by William Stoddart, 2003

Every Branch in Me: Essays on the Meaning of Man,
edited by Barry McDonald, 2002

Every Man An Artist:
Readings in the Traditional Philosophy of Art,
edited by Brian Keeble, 2005

Figures of Speech or Figures of Thought?
The Traditional View of Art,
by Ananda K. Coomaraswamy, 2007

A Guide to Hindu Spirituality, by Arvind Sharma, 2006

Introduction to Sufism: The Inner Path of Islam,
by Éric Geoffroy, 2010

Introduction to Traditional Islam, Illustrated:
Foundations, Art, and Spirituality, by Jean-Louis Michon, 2008

Islam, Fundamentalism, and the Betrayal of Tradition:
Essays by Western Muslim Scholars,
edited by Joseph E.B. Lumbard, 2004, 2009

Journeys East: 20th Century Western Encounters with
Eastern Religious Traditions, by Harry Oldmeadow, 2004

Light From the East:
Eastern Wisdom for the Modern West,
edited by Harry Oldmeadow, 2007

Living in Amida's Universal Vow:
Essays in Shin Buddhism,
edited by Alfred Bloom, 2004

Of the Land and the Spirit:
The Essential Lord Northbourne on Ecology and Religion,
edited by Christopher James and Joseph A. Fitzgerald, 2008

Paths to the Heart: Sufism and the Christian East,
edited by James S. Cutsinger, 2002

Remembering in a World of Forgetting:
Thoughts on Tradition and Postmodernism,
by William Stoddart, 2008

Returning to the Essential: Selected Writings of Jean Biès,
translated by Deborah Weiss-Dutilh, 2004

Science and the Myth of Progress,
edited by Mehrdad M. Zarandi, 2003

Seeing God Everywhere: Essays on Nature and the Sacred,
edited by Barry McDonald, 2003

Singing the Way: Insights in Poetry and Spiritual Transformation,
by Patrick Laude, 2005

The Spiritual Legacy of the North American Indian:
Commemorative Edition, by Joseph E. Brown, 2007

Sufism: Love & Wisdom,
edited by Jean-Louis Michon and Roger Gaetani, 2006

The Timeless Relevance of Traditional Wisdom,
by M. Ali Lakhani, 2010

The Underlying Religion:
An Introduction to the Perennial Philosophy,
edited by Martin Lings and Clinton Minnaar, 2007

Unveiling the Garden of Love: Mystical Symbolism in Layla
Majnun and Gita Govinda, by Lalita Sinha, 2008

Wisdom's Journey: Living the Spirit of Islam in the Modern World,
by John Herlihy, 2009

Ye Shall Know the Truth: Christianity and the
Perennial Philosophy, edited by Mateus Soares de Azevedo, 2005